TWENTY TALES
OF IRISH SAINTS

ALICE CURTAYNE

TWENTY TALES OF IRISH SAINTS

SOPHIA INSTITUTE PRESS®
Manchester, New Hampshire

Twenty Tales of Irish Saints was originally published by Sheed and Ward (New York: 1955). This 2004 edition by Sophia Institute Press® contains new illustrations, additional biographical material, and minor editorial revisions to the original text.

Sophia Institute Press®
Box 5284, Manchester, NH 03108
1-800-888-9344
www.sophiainstitute.com

Nihil obstat:
Rev. Thomas J. McHugh, L.L.D.
Censor Librorum

Imprimatur:
Jerome D. Hannan
Bishop of Scranton
June 16, 1955

Library of Congress Cataloging-in-Publication Data
Curtayne, Alice.
Twenty tales of Irish saints / Alice Curtayne.
    p. cm.
ISBN 1-928832-38-5 (pbk. : alk. paper)
1. Christian saints—Ireland—Biography.
2. Legends—Ireland. I. Title.
BX4659.I7C8 2004
282'.092'2415—dc22   2004000629

CONTENTS

Author's Note vii

1. Patrick 3

2. Brigid 9

3. Brendan 17

4. Finnian 25

5. Columcille 35

6. Colman of Kilmacduagh 41

7. Adamnan 49

8. Benignus 57

9. Ciaran 67

10. Cormac 75

11. Modomnoc 83

12. Flannan 91

13. Finbarr 99

14. Colman-Elo 107

15. Canice 115

16. Columbanus 121

17. Laurence O'Toole 129

18. Thaddeus MacCarthy 139

19. Gall 147

20. The Young Monk 153

     About the Saints 157

     About the Author 161

AUTHOR'S NOTE

All the stories in this book are about real people who lived long ago in Ireland. But even though these people really lived, the stories about them are just legends. Whether such things really happened or not, I am sure you will agree with me that the stories in this book are lovely, interesting, and worth knowing.

TWENTY TALES
OF IRISH SAINTS

his is a story about St. Patrick and two little princesses, Ethna and Fedelma. They were the daughters of the king of Connaught, the northwest province of Ireland. They were quite young, indeed little more than children, and full of fun and life. In the summer months, when the weather was hot, they used to begin the day with a bath. The place they bathed in was near the palace, yet it was quite private, and no one ever came near it early in the morning.

But one day Ethna and Fedelma and their two maids-in-waiting had a great surprise: they found a number of tents set up on the grassy slope near their bathing pool. They stared; then they listened.

There was a droning sound of voices speaking in a strange language. Every now and again a voice broke into song — and very sweet it was, mingled with the bird song from the nearby woods and the water sound from the river.

St. Patrick and his companions had come and were saying the Divine Office in Latin. They had arrived during the night and they brought a message for the king of Connaught. Of course they knew nothing of princesses taking daily baths, and the little princesses, because they were pagans, knew nothing at all about Patrick and his companions.

The voices stopped and a man came out into the open. He was small but strongly made. He looked like a man who spent all his days and nights in the open. It was St. Patrick. The girls and the man stared at one another. Then the older princess said, rather severely, "Who are you, and where do you come from?"

Patrick did not answer for some seconds. Then he said, "We have more important things to tell you than just our names and where we come from. We know who the one true God whom you should adore is."

Some might say that the saint did not answer the princesses very politely. He brushed aside their questions and went on to tell them something quite different. But far from being annoyed, the young girls were delighted. In a flash something seemed to light up inside them, to make a blinding white blaze in their hearts and minds. They knew at once that this was real — real news that was as true as night and day, as true as being alive. It all happened in seconds.

Then they asked questions — a whole torrent of questions.

"Who is God?"

"Where does He live?"

"Will He live forever?"

"Will we see Him and be with Him when we die?"

"Who is His Son?"

"Is Christ beautiful?"

"What are we to do?"

Quickly and simply, Patrick answered all their questions. He, too, was delighted: the light that blazed up in the girls was in the man, too, and those three lights together made a tremendous glow. The maids and Patrick's companions stood around listening to the quick questions and the lovely answers. They knew that they were very lucky to be near the saintly man and the sweet girls and they felt that the Holy Spirit was there, too, in their midst.

"Oh, tell us how to find the good God. Teach us more about the kind Christ who died on the cross. Tell us more, more, more," the two princesses urged.

But there was no great need to tell more: they had already received the Spirit of Truth. Patrick led them to the pool where each morning they went to bathe and there he baptized them. For a little while after, Ethna and Fedelma were very still. They asked no more questions; they were praying. Patrick prepared to say Mass. His companions made the altar ready. Then the girls came to him again.

"I want to *see* Jesus Christ now," said Ethna.

"And so do I," said Fedelma. "I want to be with Him in His home for ever and ever."

Patrick was very moved by this loving longing. Very gently he explained to them that it was impossible, they would not be able to see God until after death. They were still young, he told them, and they had their lives to live. If they lived good Christian lives, they would then be able to go to God for always and always and great joys would take the place of the sorrows of this world. The girls said no more and Patrick began the Mass.

The Mass went on. The water seemed to sing as it flowed by, an odd bird chirruped, a wind rustled the leaves in the trees. Everyone was still. Then the youngest man in the company rang a little bell and all bowed their heads. Jesus Christ was with them in that grassy place beside the water in the king of Connaught's park. Soon the bell rang again: it was the Communion of the Mass. Patrick turned around with the vessel of Sacred Hosts and, beckoning to the king's daughters, he gave them Holy Communion.

For a little while the girls looked so happy and so beautiful that they were like angels. And then (the story tells us) they died. They longed so much to be with Christ that they died of longing. We don't know — and we will never know until we die ourselves — why God took those young girls, but He must have loved them very much to have done so. We do know, however, how happy St. Patrick was to have met with such quick, wholehearted, whole-souled belief.

When he had to take the road again — the hard unkind road that went up and down Ireland — his step was light and there was a smile on his lips.

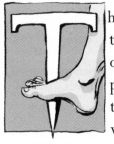here were only two being baptized in the Ethna and Fedelma story, but often Patrick baptized hundreds of people on a single day. He would come to a place, a crowd would gather, and when he told them about the true God, the people would cry out from all sides that they wanted to become Christians. Then all would move off to the nearest river, or well, to be baptized.

It was that way when Aengus was baptized. He was a Prince of Munster and when St. Patrick finished preaching, Aengus was longing with all his heart to become a Christian. The crowd surrounded Patrick as he prepared to baptize this important man. Patrick got out his book and began to look for the place of the baptismal ceremony but he found that his crosier was in his way.

A bishop always carries a crosier about with him. A bishop is a shepherd not of sheep, of course, but of people. A shepherd carries a crook, which is a long stick with a curved top, while a bishop carries a crosier, which is nothing more than a rather ornamental crook.

Very often crosiers have spikes at their ends, I suppose so that they may be stuck in the ground if the bishop has to do something else with his hands.

Patrick's crosier had a metal spike on the end of it, and, when he began to search for the place in his book so that he could baptize Aengus, he stuck his crosier into the ground just beside him. But the crosier didn't go into the ground; it went instead right through poor Aengus's foot!

Patrick, never noticing what he had done, went on with the ceremony. The prince did not cry out, or even moan; he went very white and that was all.

Patrick poured the water over Aengus's bowed head, saying, "In the Name of the Father, and of the Son, and of the Holy Spirit." It was over; Aengus was a Christian. Patrick turned to take up his crosier and was horrified to find that he had driven the sharp spike through the prince's foot.

"But why didn't you say something! This is terrible. Your foot is bleeding and you'll be lame. . . ." Poor St. Patrick was very unhappy.

In a low voice, Aengus said that he thought having a spike driven through his foot was part of the ceremony. Then Aengus added something which must have brought joy to the whole court of Heaven and blessings on Ireland, "Christ shed His blood for me, and I am glad to suffer a little pain at Baptism to be like our Lord."

t. Brigid was a great saint and Irish people are very proud of her. She had a way about her that's hard to explain. Country people (or at least the people in our part of the country, which happens to be Brigid's, too) often say, when telling you about somebody outstanding and independent, "Ah, sure, he's himself," or, "Ah, sure, she's herself." Well, St. Brigid was herself.

There was no one like her. She got things done; she had a great welcome for everyone; she was so generous that she'd give away the clothes off her back; she was a great one for hard work and also for long prayers; she would brush aside rules — even some Church rules — if it was necessary to make people happy and comfortable; she said a lot of "do's" but hardly any "don'ts."

Brigid saw the beauty and goodness of God in everything: even cows made her love God more, and wild duck did, too. Yes, wild duck used to come to her when she called them; they would alight on her shoulders and hands without any fear. That, you must admit, was very strange because if any creature deserves to be called wild, it is a wild duck. Usually wild duck hate the sight of men and are happy only when miles away from people.

hen there was the time she saved the wild boar. Here is the story. First you must know about something called sanctuary. In olden times the ground enclosed as a monastery, or convent, by monks, or nuns, was considered holy ground; it was a sacred place where God was worshiped. If a bad man, even a thief or a murderer, was trying to escape from being put into prison, he would be safe if he once reached a monastery or convent. He was then in sanctuary and no one could do anything to him until he himself agreed to leave.

Well, the wild animals seemed to know about this law, too.

One day a wild boar that was being chased by hunters was on the point of being caught. (In the old days wild pigs were chased as well as foxes and deer.) The boar just managed to reach St. Brigid's convent in Kildare; the hunters drew up outside the gate and waited. They expected the nuns to chase the boar out to them again and then they could easily kill it. But they didn't know Brigid; she was herself and had her own ideas about most things. She happened to see the unhappy boar staggering in, so she called it to her and then sent a message out to the horsemen, saying that they could not have it because animals had the right of sanctuary in her convent just as much as people had.

They sent back a message saying that animals were only animals and had not the same rights as men, and could they have their boar, please. And she sent back a final message saying that as far as her land was concerned, animals did have the right of sanctuary on it, just like people.

That was the last word. The disappointed hunters rode away. Then Brigid turned her attention to the poor boar; it was lying down, exhausted from its long run and nearly frightened to death. She gave it a drink and then led it to her own herd of pigs. At once the wild boar became quite tame and settled down with the other pigs on Brigid's farm for the rest of its life.

f all the Irish saints who had a way with animals Brigid was the best. She could even train a wild fox to do tricks.

One day some working men came to Brigid with a sad story: a friend of theirs had been cutting down trees in the king of Leinster's woods when he saw a fox nearby. He thought it was a wild fox and, flinging a stone at it, killed it instantly. But he was mistaken: it was a tame fox and the king's favorite pet.

The king heard the news when the dead fox was carried back to the palace. He was furiously angry and didn't delay a minute before sending soldiers to arrest the man. As soon as the prisoner was brought before him, the king sentenced him to death. The man's wife and children begged the king to change his mind. They said that it was a mistake, that no one could have known whether the fox was wild or tame, but the king would not listen to them. The man was to die and that was the end of it.

"Will you come, please?" the man's friends begged Brigid. "Talk to the king. He will listen to you. Save our friend."

Although Brigid loved animals, she thought it very silly that a man's life should be demanded in return for a fox's. She was always getting appeals like this, and always answering them. She immediately told one of her own workmen to bring around her chariot and she set out in it for the king's castle.

The way lay through a wood, where the road was a mere track and the horse had to walk. Brigid prayed as she went along that she would think of the right things to say to the angry king so as to save the woodsman, whose wife and children were so unhappy.

Suddenly she saw a little fox peeping shyly at her around a tree and she had an idea. She told the driver to stop and she called the animal to her. Immediately the fox trotted up, sprang into the chariot beside her, and nestled happily in the folds of her cloak. Brigid stroked its head and spoke to it gently. The little fox licked her hand and looked at her adoringly.

When she reached the king's castle, the fox trotted after her. She found the ruler still in a mighty rage. "Nothing," he told her angrily, "nothing in the world could make up to me for the loss of my beloved pet. Death is too good for that idiot of a workman. He must die as a warning to others like him. Let him die."

The king stormed on, "It is no use whining to me about mercy. That little fox was my companion, even my friend. It was brutally killed for no reason. What harm did I do to that man? Do you have any notion how much I loved my little fox that I had cared for ever since it was born?"

The king's furious eyes met Brigid's loving ones. Yes, indeed, she could well understand it. She was truly sorry for his loss — she, too, loved all animals, especially little tame foxes. Look here . . . she beckoned forward her new pet that had been crouching behind her.

The king forgot his anger in this new interest. He and his household watched delightedly while Brigid proceeded to put the fox through all kinds of clever tricks. It obeyed her voice and tried so hard to please her that the onlookers were greatly entertained. Soon she was surrounded by laughing faces.

The king told her what his own little fox used to do, "See, it used to jump through this hoop, even at this height." But so could Brigid's fox at her first sign of command. When the king's fox wanted a tidbit, it used to stand on its hind legs with its forepaws joined as though it were praying — why, so could Brigid's. Could anything be more amusing? When his mood had completely changed, Brigid offered her fox to the king in exchange for the prisoner's life. Now the king smilingly agreed and he even promised Brigid that never again would he inflict any kind of punishment on that workman, whose misdeed he would forget.

Brigid was very happy when the prisoner was finally restored to his wife and children. She went back home, thanking God.

But the little fox missed her sorely and became restless and unhappy. It did not care where Brigid led him but, without her, the castle was a prison. After a while the king went off on some business and no one else bothered very much about the new pet. The fox watched for its chance and when it found a door open, it made good its escape back to the wood.

Presently the king returned and what a commotion there was when the fox was missed. The whole household was sent out to search for it.

When they failed, the king's hounds were sent to help in the search, their keen noses snuffling over the ground for the fox's scent. Then the excited king summoned out his whole army, both horsemen and footmen to follow the hounds in every direction.

But it was all of no use. When night fell, the hosts of Leinster returned wearily to their king with news of failure. Brigid's little fox was never found again.

t. Brendan is the boast of County Kerry. A great mountain that juts out into the Atlantic Ocean there is called Mount Brandon after him, because he had a little chapel on the top of it, and the bay at the foot of that mountain is called Brandon Bay.

When he became a priest, he had an idea of his own: he thought he would travel the world and find new lands to which he could bring the good news of the Gospel. That is why he is called Brendan the Navigator. He was the first sailor-saint of Ireland.

He was a long time preparing for such tremendous journeys. First he got men to help him make a great boat out of the trunk of a giant oak tree. It was manned by twenty men, ten down each side, each of them having an oar.

This was the sixth century, before compasses or steam engines had been invented, and there were very few maps of the known world. So Brendan had to depend on the sun and the stars to find his way and on the wind to make speed. They would have to row the boat on days when there was no wind.

When the boat was ready, lots of food had to be packed into it, for Brendan knew that he might be months sometimes without coming in sight of land.

Brendan's companions were all monks like himself and they made up their minds that they would keep the monastic rules as strictly as if they were still living on land, so that they had a kind of a floating monastery.

They were all sailors as well as monks and most of the time they found their journeys great fun and very interesting. But sometimes, when they were weeks and weeks without seeing land, they got tired and a little frightened. And they were often downright terrified in storms, or when their lives were in danger, all except Brendan.

Brendan was never afraid. He was absolutely positive all the time that God would not let anything happen to him. He just did not seem to know what it meant to be afraid.

ne beautiful summer's day, they were floating gently over the water, which was as smooth and clear as a sheet of glass. There was just enough breeze to carry the boat along and everyone was

very happy. Brendan reminded them that it was the feast of St. Paul and that they should celebrate that high day with special devotion and glory. So every kind of work on the boat was laid aside while they all sang the Office together.

Brendan's voice was particularly sweet and ringing and he led the others. Some of his companions happened to glance down at the sea while they were singing and they noticed a strange excitement going on around their boat. On every side of it, fish beyond counting were rising in vast numbers to the surface.

They looked in alarm at Brendan, but he was singing away, not seeming to notice anything. All at once the monks felt terrified. They had never before in their lives seen such numbers of fish all at once and they thought the singing had annoyed them and that the fish might capsize the boat.

They interrupted their prayers to tell Brendan, "Sing more quietly, Master, or we shall surely be shipwrecked."

But Brendan "laughed a great laugh" at them and told them they were being foolish. The great prayer went on, and the fish gamboled and sported near the surface of the water all the time that the Office was being sung. The moment it ended, they sank once more into the depths of the sea.

The Abbot was right; the fish had risen to the surface because they liked the prayers.

nother day, the sailor-monks from Kerry landed on a beautiful little island, full of flowers and fruit.

Since it was so small, they decided to walk across it; and what do you think they found in the middle of it but a little church built of stone and a holy old man saying his prayers before the altar?

The monks were delighted, but not so the old man. He said they must hurry away at once because there was a dreadful monster on the island, a huge sea cat that killed every stranger who landed on it; it never did the old man any harm, but no one else was safe from it.

When the sailors heard this news, they got very nervous and begged Brendan to hurry back to the boat. When they reached it, they seized the oars and rowed with such a right good will that they seemed to fly through the water.

But after they had gone about a mile, they saw the dreaded monster swimming strongly after them from the island. Even at a distance they could see that it had great eyes like vessels of glass.

It came steadily nearer and nearer no matter how they tried to get away. The only one in the boat who was not afraid was Brendan; he just sat there, his lips moving in prayer, calmly gazing on the beast getting nearer and nearer to them.

Just as it had nearly reached the boat, another strange, huge, fishlike creature suddenly rose to the surface of the water and attacked the sea cat. There was a terrible fight and the sea was soon reddened with blood.

The sailors rested on their oars and watched, fascinated, as the two animals threshed round and round in mortal combat. Suddenly both of them sank out of sight, never to be seen again.

Thanking God for their delivery, the sailors again turned back to the island and once more sought out the old man at his prayers. He was very pleased at their news. Then he told them that he, too, had come from Ireland many years before with twelve companions. They had brought with them a little kitten which got the habit of eating nothing but fish and gradually grew into the monster they had seen. As the years went by, his companions had died one by one and now he, an old man, was waiting for God to take him too.

They then decided to rest on the island for some days. Brendan gave the old man the Sacraments, which he had not been able to receive for a very long time.

The old man was so happy after Holy Communion that they suspected he was dying, so Brendan gave him the Last Rites, too, and he died that day.

They buried him beside his little church. He had lived such a good life that they were sure God had brought them to him in answer to his prayers.

ome weeks later, Brendan and his companions landed on yet another island. As they moored their boat, the first thing they saw was a tree of strange height covered with snowy white birds, singing so beautifully that they were all enraptured. They sat down under the tree, staring and listening, unable either to speak or to go away.

Presently one of the dazzling birds flew down from the tree and perched on the highest part of the prow of the boat. It looked at Brendan so intently that the saint knew it wished to speak. He asked it to tell him what the birds were, and the strange creature answered in human language that they were the souls of angels who had wavered for an instant at the great rebellion in Heaven, when Michael the Archangel had cast out all the fallen angels. Because these particular angels had not actually rebelled against God, but had only been uncertain for a moment, they had been sent to this island.

"Here," the bird told Brendan, "On the solemn feasts and on the Sabbaths, we take such bodies as ye see. We know no other pain than that we cannot see the presence of God."

That night the sailors were enchanted to hear the birds sing the whole of the Divine Office. The travelers stayed on this holy island as long as they could and "the sweet singing of the birds was their delight and their reviving."

When Brendan returned to Ireland from his voyages, the stories of his adventures were so wonderful that people everywhere crowded around him to hear about his travels. They wrote down the stories, too, so that they would never be forgotten and also because people outside Ireland wanted to hear them.

These tales were told all over Europe in succeeding centuries, and Brendan the Navigator became one of the best known of the Irish saints. He is a very good person to pray to if ever you happen to be afraid of anything.

innian was born at Myshall in County Carlow, during the fifth century, while St. Patrick was still alive and teaching the Faith to the Irish people. Finnian's parents were from Ulster.

From his childhood he wanted to go into the Church and he had made up his mind very early about what exactly he wanted to do (and that is nearly always halfway toward being what a boy wants to be). Finnian did not want to be a missionary and go away to foreign countries; he did not want to be a hermit and live in a forest, or on an island; he wanted to be a teacher.

He certainly went about it the right way. First he studied for a much longer time than anyone studies nowadays. Then when he knew all that could be taught to him in Ireland, he went to a famous school in Wales, where he met many great Welsh churchmen like David and Gildas.

He was not long in this great school before his teachers noticed that he was not quite like other boys. He had an extraordinary memory, to begin with, and he could remember everything that he had read once. He learned quickly and without effort.

But that wasn't all. Strange things used to happen when Finnian was around; things that one could not altogether explain. So soon all the teachers were saying that this boy was favored by God and he was bound to be a great man and probably a saint.

A new church was being built when Finnian joined the school. It was to be made of timber and would hold all the many students. The Abbot of this monastic school was most anxious to get the building finished, and for some weeks he let the students off lessons to help the working men at drawing fallen trees from the woods. But he did not send Finnian out because he thought Finnian was better employed at his books.

One of the younger masters, or teachers, at this school was a bit jealous that Finnian was excused from the hard work of sawing and dragging timber. Indeed, he thought that there was altogether too much fuss made of this Irish student.

So he went to where Finnian was studying one morning and said roughly, "Why aren't you out in the woods with the other boys?"

"I was not told to go," answered Finnian.

"Told or not told, you should be out with them and working."

Finnian considered this for a moment. Then he said, "Do you wish me to go?"

"Yes, certainly," said the master.

"Well, where shall I find a yoke of oxen now?" Finnian knew that by this time no animal was left around the monastery and that without any oxen he could not bring home his load. And the master knew that, too.

"There are deer outside," jeered the unpleasant master. "Can't you catch a couple and make them pull your load?"

Poor Finnian put away his books, which he loved, and went off to do as he was told. But he was thinking sadly that he was going to have trouble. "That's a hard one, and no mistake. How are deer to be caught? They stand still for no man and I can't expect to get them in a trap even if I were to set a trap at once." He imagined himself spending the rest of the day chasing deer around the countryside and not getting within yards of them.

Nevertheless he set off on his difficult job looking for deer. It was likely to go on all day, but then something happened, one of the strange things that often happened when he was around.

Very shortly after Finnian set out, he saw a young man leading two stags which seemed to be just as tame as pet ponies. The man led them up to Finnian and before the astonished boy could speak, he disappeared. It was an angel sent to help Finnian as a reward for his obedience.

Finnian yoked the stags to a timber cart and took them to the place where the men and students were felling trees. The stags worked so well that even though he had made such a late start, he was the first to get back to the monastery with his load of timber for the new church.

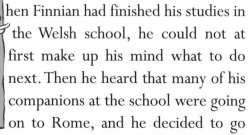hen Finnian had finished his studies in the Welsh school, he could not at first make up his mind what to do next. Then he heard that many of his companions at the school were going on to Rome, and he decided to go with them. He thought it would be a wonderful thing to see the Pope and to learn more about the Church and religion in the very center of Christianity.

He had just made up his mind when one night an angel appeared to him. "Go back to Ireland," the angel said. "You are needed there."

"But Rome," said Finnian sadly, "how I long to go there!"

"Whatever you are seeking in Rome, you will find it in Ireland," said the angel; so Finnian obeyed and went back to Ireland.

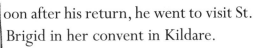 oon after his return, he went to visit St. Brigid in her convent in Kildare.

There were two monasteries in Kildare at that time: one for monks and the other for nuns. The monks did the most wonderful metalwork. They made all sorts of objects for church use: chalices, patens, Mass book stands, Tabernacle doors, and many other things like that.

Brigid was famous for her kindness to visitors. As soon as Finnian had had a good dinner and a rest, she took him around the place and showed him every-thing: her own cows, sheep, and dairy, and also the metalworks in the monastery next door.

All the while she was puzzling in her own mind about what present she would give him when he was leaving. It was her nice way — indeed, everyone's nice way in those times — to give an honored guest some little parting gift at the end of a visit.

While they were looking at the lovely things being made by the metalworkers, Brigid picked up a gold ring. She told Finnian to try it on. It fit him perfectly.

"Keep it," said Brigid. "It's yours."

"No, no," Finnian said. "I couldn't possibly take it."

"Oh, but you must," said Brigid, quite determined.

"Oh, but I must not," said Finnian, waving her off and getting a little cross. "I've made a vow of poverty, you know. I don't want anything to do with gold."

"I know all that," said Brigid, "but I tell you to take this ring because you will need it soon."

"Thank you very much indeed," said Finnian, but not very politely now. "Monks have no business with rings and I won't take it."

They were both strong-minded people and the argument lasted quite a while. Brigid wouldn't give up; she seemed to have some very good reason Finnian should have the ring. "You'll want this ring before many days are over. Take it, I tell you."

"No," said Finnian obstinately.

He went off without the ring, but of course they parted good friends all the same. Finnian thanked Brigid for all her kindness and she wished him every good luck and blessing in the school he intended to set up.

He then had to go a long journey. It was a warm summer day and presently he got very hot, dusty, and sticky. When he came to a river, he was glad to sit down for a while and watch its cool sparkle. After a time he washed his hands in the running water and what did he see on one of his fingers but Brigid's gold ring! He was amazed; he couldn't believe his eyes. He was absolutely sure and positive that he had not taken the ring from her hand.

"Well," he said, smiling to himself, "there's no getting away from Brigid when she makes up her mind to do something." By the time he made the discovery he was much too far from Kildare to think of going back with the ring, so he just had to keep it.

Toward evening, he fell in with a young man who was taking the same road and they stepped along together. Soon they became very friendly. The stranger's name was Caisin and he told Finnian all about himself. He said that he had a longing to become a priest if only he could meet with someone who would help him.

"What kind of help do you need?" asked Finnian.

Caisin explained that he was living in the king of Leinster's castle; he didn't want to live there but was being held as a hostage. Therefore, before he could leave, he must buy his freedom.

"What does the king want in return for your freedom?" asked Finnian.

"Gold," said Caisin sadly.

Finnian was just about to say that of course he had no gold when, with a start, he remembered Brigid's ring.

"How much gold do you want?" he asked.

"I think a very little would do — even an ounce," answered the youth.

Finnian then showed him the ring on his finger and said that he would be delighted to give it to the king if it was enough. So they decided to turn aside from their road and go at once to the king of Leinster's castle.

When they arrived the ring was weighed and it was found to be exactly right. The king gave Caisin his freedom. Caisin never again left Finnian. When he, too, became a priest, he was a great help to Finnian in setting up his schools.

Good teachers make good schools. Finnian was a great teacher who started the great school of Clonard. There was no question on the Gospel you could possibly ask him that he could not answer. But teaching is only one thing; there is another means of making good men out of boys: showing them a way of life.

Finnian showed a wonderful example in the hard way he lived; he always slept on the ground with a stone for a pillow. His food on ordinary days was black barley bread and water, and on Sundays and holy days he feasted by eating wheaten bread, broiled salmon, and mead, a drink made from honey.

If Finnian himself had to go to Wales to study, no Irishman after him had to do so because they had Clonard, which was soon better than the best schools in Britain. It drew pupils from all over the Christian world and sometimes there were as many as three thousand pupils under Finnian's rule.

Many of these pupils became great men afterward: twelve saints came out of it (they were known as the Twelve Apostles of Ireland) and a countless number became bishops and famous churchmen.

It was, indeed, Clonard that began what was known as the Golden Age, something that never again happened in Irish Church history. For three hundred years, at least, missionaries poured out of Ireland, carrying the Faith to the ends of what was then the known world. The power to do such great things came from Finnian's Clonard and the good and holy man who lived there.

reland has so many saints they are practically countless — and three great ones. The great ones are Patrick, Brigid, and Columcille. These three are like sparkling jewels in a crown and it would be hard to say which sparkled the most; perhaps it would depend on the light in which you looked at the jewels.

In one light, at any rate, Columcille sparkles the brightest: Irishness. He loved Ireland with all his might, even though he left Ireland for the little island of Iona, near the bigger island Mull, off the west coast of Scotland. He was also very Irish in himself: he had a quick temper, yet he was very kind, especially to children and animals; he was a poet and an artist who did scroll work such as one sees in the Book of Kells (some think he did part of the work in that Book himself); and he even looked Irish.

We have a description of his appearance which begins this way: "A man well formed, with powerful frame; his skin was white, his face broad and fair and radiant, lit up with large, gray, luminous eyes. . . ."

Columcille's heart was always touched when he saw a sad child. Now and again he used to leave Iona to preach Christianity to the Scots, or Picts, as they were called in those times. Once when he was visiting a Pictish king, he noticed a thin little girl with a face like a ghost. He asked who she was and was told that she was just a slave from Ireland.

The way it was said seemed to mean, "Why do you ask such silly questions? Who cares who she is, as long as she brushes and scrubs and does what she is told?" But Columcille was troubled; he could see plainly that the little girl was miserable.

So he asked the king to give the girl her freedom and promised that he would himself take care of getting her home to Ireland. The king refused, and Columcille went away with a picture of the unhappy little girl in his mind.

Shortly afterward, the Pictish king became ill; there was nobody nearby to tell him what to do to get well so he sent for the Abbot of Iona, who had a great reputation for curing people. Columcille did not leave Iona but instead sent back a message that he would cure the king if he let the little girl free. The king was angry and again refused.

"What on earth is he troubling himself for about that little bit of a good-for-nothing?" grumbled the king as he tossed about in bed. But the messenger had hardly left for Iona with the refusal when the king got worse; he had so much pain that he thought he would die. So he sent off another message to Columcille, "Yes, you can have the slave girl, only come and do something for me. I am very bad and will die if you don't come soon."

Perhaps you think that the next thing you will hear is that Columcille immediately set off with his medicines and never stopped until he reached the king's house. No, he did not. He was afraid that this man was not to be trusted and might say one thing and do another. So Columcille first sent two of his monks to the house with instructions to bring the little Irish girl back to Iona. And this they did.

When the girl was safe, Columcille set out for the king's house and cured him of his sickness. After a while they got the little girl away to Ireland where, no doubt, she lived happily ever after.

ow Columcille wished he could go back to Ireland himself! His heart was always aching for his own country and living away from it in Iona was penance for him. But he put God's work before his own wishes and spreading the Faith was the thing that came first and counted most.

Besides sending back a poor little Cinderella girl, Columcille also sent back a bird. One day a stork came winging to Iona from the direction of Ireland; it dropped down on the strand and appeared to be terribly exhausted. Columcille called two of his monks and they went down to the strand to the stork. The bird was so tired that it did not try to get away. They lifted it gently and carried it tenderly back to the monastery and then for three days they fed it and nursed it.

"You must make it well," said Columcille to the monk who had charge of the sick, "so that it may return to its sweet home in Ireland, whence it came." It was with great joy — and yet a sort of sad joy — that Columcille watched the stork open its big wings and take off for Ireland.

One of the monks standing by asked, "Why were you so fond of that bird?"

"Because," said Columcille, "it came from my homeland."

Perhaps he wrote a poem that day because the stork made him feel homesick and a great many of his poems are homesick ones. Here is a verse from his poem about leaving Ireland:

How swiftly we travel! There is a gray eye
Looks back upon Erin, but it no more
Shall see while the stars shall endure in the sky,
Her women, her men, or her stainless shore.

hen Columcille was seventy-six years of age, he said one day that he was going to die in a week's time.

Everyone was astonished! He was still so strong and he never had had any sort of serious illness. But he was certain that the time had come for going, so each morning of that week he went the round of the monastery examining everything: he went through the workshops, walked every field of the farm, and then looked into the supplies in the kitchens and storehouses.

While on this round, Columcille bade farewell to all: monks, lay brothers, servants, working boys.

There was great sorrow for he was very much loved — loved more than the commander of an army or the captain of a ship. Columcille was that sort of a man: a leader, a man other men looked up to and wanted to be like.

There is an old Irish Song of Praise which gives a list of all Columcille's goodness; if you were to read it you would certainly say, "This is the kind of man I would love, too, and I, too, would be sad if I knew he was soon to die."

On the last day of Columcille's life, he went out to the middle of the island and blessed it and all who lived on it. He looked so strong and well that no one could really believe that he was to die.

On his way back from blessing the island, he sat down near the farm buildings for a rest. An old white horse slowly trotted out to him.

This horse was a favorite of Columcille's: every morning and evening for more than twenty years it had brought the milk from the cow byres to the monastery. When the poor animal reached the man it began to whinny in the most heartbreaking way. Columcille called it to him and stroked its long bony nose, pressing it tight against his breast.

There was a monk with the Abbot and he wanted to drive the old horse away, but Columcille would not allow him. For quite a while the horse remained, tears rolling out of its old eyes and mournful sounds coming from it. Then Columcille blessed it — just as he blessed the monks and the others — and went away to his cell.

For the rest of the day he wrote in beautiful lettering just as he delighted to do every ordinary day. He was prepared for death and he wasn't worried or excited. That night he died in the church at the foot of the altar.

Columcille was first buried in Iona, but two hundred years later, after some wicked Danes came and smashed up the monastery, his body was brought back to Ireland. And so it will rest in his beloved Ireland until the Last Day when all bodies and souls will be united for all eternity.

 lmost every child in the world has kept a pet of some kind. St. Colman of Kilmacduagh is a man whom those children will like and who will like them. He was the first bishop of the diocese of Galway and Kilmacduagh and it is more than fourteen hundred years since he lived his holy, simple life in south Galway.

Colman loved birds and animals. When he lived at Kilmacduagh, he had a pet rooster which used to come and eat out of his hand and then perch on his shoulder as he walked about the monastery garden.

In those days there were no clocks such as we have now and people knew the time just by watching the sun and by other simple means. Colman found his pet rooster most useful; it acted as a clock for him. It would come to the window of his cell at daylight and crow and crow, not stopping until Colman came out and spoke to it. The rooster's crowing meant that night was over and the first light was appearing in the sky. It was time to get up and ring the bell and rouse the rest of the monks. The rooster was far more useful to the monks than any alarm clock — and they could make a pet of the rooster.

Colman and the holy monks who lived with him did not think it enough to get up at dawn to begin their prayers. They wanted to get up in the middle of the night, too, for an hour's praying; they believed in the power of prayer to change the world.

ut how were the monks to be awakened during the night? It was the rooster's sleeping time; he couldn't be expected to keep guard day and night. In a corner of his cell, Colman noticed a mouse peeping out at him now and again when he got up in the night to pray. He made a pet of this little creature, giving it crumbs and tidbits. After a while the mouse became quite tame and used to run to Colman the moment he heard him stirring.

Soon Colman began to talk to the mouse. He would say, "So you are awake all night, are you? It isn't your time for sleep, is it? My friend, the rooster, gives me great help, waking me every morning. Couldn't you do the same for me at night, while the rooster is asleep? If you do not find me stirring at the usual time, couldn't you call me? Will you do that?" The mouse would look up at Colman with its little beady eyes as if it understood what he was saying.

However, Colman did not put it to the test for a very long time, because in truth he was really quite good at waking during the night whenever he wanted. But one day he had to go a long distance from his monastery to preach a special sermon for a new church. He made the entire journey on foot, so he was very tired when he got to his cell that night and he slept like a log. When the time came for Colman to be up and praying, he was still fast asleep. Out ran the mouse to greet his friend in the usual way, but there was no smiling man to give him crumbs and dainties this time, only the sound of gentle breathing as Colman slept on and on.

The mouse pattered over to the bed and then all at once understood what was expected of him. He climbed up on the pillow and rubbed his tiny head against Colman's ear. The sleeping man only sighed and turned over to the wall. The mouse followed the ear and rubbed it a little harder this time. Colman shook his head impatiently. But the mouse knew well what was his job and he nibbled the ear. That did it. Colman sprang straight out of bed, because he had the habits of a soldier and always got up in a flash. Then he saw the little mouse and he burst out laughing. The mouse, very serious and important, just sat there looking at him. Colman laughed and laughed, and every time he looked at the mouse sitting on the pillow, he had to laugh again. "So you took it in all right? You understood what I was telling you," he said.

Well, when he had finished his great laugh, you may be sure Colman got extra crumbs for his pet and probably a little bit of cheese, too. He praised the mouse highly for being so clever, faithful, and useful. Then he had another laugh, and then he began his prayers — monks are like that, good at laughing and extra good at praying.

Every night after that, Colman, even when he was awake, would wait for the mouse to rub his ear before he got up. The mouse never failed him, but exactly at two o'clock, would wake his master.

Animals know the time perfectly and they are much better than clocks because they don't go fast or slow or stop altogether. Colman used to tell his friends how rich and happy he was, having a friend to wake him during the night and another to call him at dawn.

olman had even a stranger pet than a rooster or a mouse: it was a fly. In those days, they didn't have printed books with covers on them such as we have. Their books — probably you wouldn't call them books at all — were written by hand on large sheets of parchment.

When Colman was reading his prayers out of one of those large awkward books, a fly would come every day and perch on the margin.

Presently Colman knew the fly quite well and when he had finished his prayers, he would talk to it.

"I like your company very much," he would say. "You're a handsome little fellow. Thank you for staying with me like this every day. But now that you like coming, and you know that I like having you, don't you think you could do something useful for me? You see yourself that everyone who lives in the monastery is useful. Well, if I am called away, as I often am, while I am reading, don't you go, too; stay here on the spot I mark with my finger, so that I'll know exactly where to start when I come back. Do you see what I mean?"

And the shiny black fly with the big roving eyes seemed to understand.

Just as in the case of the mouse, it was a long time before Colman put the fly to the test, and he probably gave it many little dainties, too — perhaps a single drop of honey, or a crumb of cake — to encourage it to be useful and to work for the good of the monastery like everyone else.

Then one day, right in the middle of his prayers, Colman was called to see a visitor.

There was the faithful fly as usual on the margin of the book. Colman put his finger on the spot where he had stopped and said to the fly, "Now, you mark the place for me here and don't move until I come back."

The fly did as it was told, and when Colman came back an hour later, there was the obedient little thing still marking the place. Colman was delighted; he saw that the fly was going to save much time. Instead of trying to find the place on the long page where he left off, he could begin at once.

Many a time after that, Colman would stop in the middle of his prayers, even when he was not called away at all, just to give the faithful fly a little task that it was proud to do for him. And he would call the other monks in the monastery to come with him and look at the fly holding the place for him. They thought it such a marvel that they wrote it down in the monastery books and that is how we know about it today.

But a fly's life is very short; indeed it is only one summer. One day, as winter was coming on, the fly did not come, and Colman guessed what had happened: the little creature's life was over. Poor Colman felt so lonely he could hardly say his prayers. He missed his friend the fly more than I could possibly explain to you.

Mice have a rather longer life, but the night came, too, when Colman's mouse did not come out of its corner to rub his ear. He knew what had happened; he knew that he could now sleep on and on without his faithful little friend to call him. He found it very hard that day not to be sad, for he had enjoyed the mouse and loved him.

The rooster was the pet he had longest, but after six or seven years, it, too, died of old age. Colman was very put out at the loss of his last pet and he wrote to his great friend, St. Columcille, to ease his heavy heart. He told him in the letter all about those three friends of his whom he had loved so much. Columcille answered, "You were too rich when you had them. That is why you are sad now. Trouble like that only comes where there are riches. Be rich no more." I wonder did St. Colman smile, as you are smiling now, at this idea of a rooster, a mouse, and a fly making riches?

Anyhow he never again kept another pet because he did not want to be what St. Columcille called rich and he did not want to be sad when his pets died.

Well, that's the end of my story. Perhaps you would say a prayer to St. Colman of Kilmacduagh to bless the pet you have. Is it a dog or, perhaps, a kitten? I don't know, but I am pretty sure it is not a fly.

here is no use crying over spilt milk. Crying never did a bit of good, but sometimes something else can be done and little Adamnan did that something once with very good results.

Adamnan lived in Donegal and he is the patron saint of Raphoe, a diocese which contains that beautiful county. He lived a long time ago — in the seventh century. I hate bothering you with centuries and dates and I don't ask you to remember them. The only thing you need remember is that Ireland had a Golden Age when there were more holy people and wise people in our country than in any other country in the world. Adamnan lived in that Golden Age.

One day, when he was quite small, he was walking along a country road or horse track. He carried on his back a huge vessel of milk and an adventure befell him which made a great difference to the whole of his life.

I'll explain why Adamnan carried milk on his back, but I don't think I need to explain about children running errands.

Here where we live, we cannot go out our front gate without seeing either little Katy Next-door going off to the village with a shopping bag to get bread and sugar, or little Sean going off to the bog for a bag of dry turf, or little Michael carrying a bucket of water. Country children are always trotting off getting things for their parents or grandparents.

Well, little Michael now has a handy metal bucket in which to bring home water, but Adamnan had no such things. He had an earthenware jar instead. (Earthenware is just baked clay and is as easily broken as china.) This jar was very large and had a wide mouth; it was also very heavy and the only way he could carry it was to wind hay-rope around its neck, sling it on his back, and hold the tails of rope.

Adamnan's jar was filled with milk. He walked slowly and carefully because he did not want to spill a single drop; it had cost a lot of trouble to collect all that milk. You see, he went from house to house collecting it: a big bowl of it in a rich farmer's house, a small cup of it in a poor man's house. Nobody had refused when he had asked politely for a little milk and explained why he wanted it.

He wanted it for three bigger boys who were learning to be priests and who had to work at their books all day with no time to spare for collecting food. Adamnan did all the errands for these boys.

Perhaps this sounds a strange way of doing things. Well, long ago in Ireland the great schools were great men, not great buildings — if you understand.

Wherever there was a wonderful teacher like Ciaran or Finnian, pupils collected around him to learn all they could. That was the important thing: where they were to sleep and eat did not seem to worry them at all. Two or three of them would club together and put up a hut to sleep in and then find somebody kindly, like little Adamnan, to collect food for them. The great thing was to learn: it was what they came for, and they were quite happy living all the year round like boys on a camping holiday.

You needn't worry about the people who supplied the students with free food: they were pleased to be of help. In fact nearly everyone in Ireland at that time had the same idea: they wanted to spread the Catholic Faith by having more and more priests to preach it.

Adamnan was delighted with himself. He would get great praise from the three older boys for collecting so much milk and they would have plenty for drinking, for putting on their porridge, and for making puddings. Good food makes it easier to study. Adamnan thought it a grand thing to study and to be a priest. He meant to do exactly the same himself when he was old enough.

Well, he was smiling to himself as he walked along and thinking of the cheers he would get when he reached the hut. Suddenly he heard the noise of horses galloping behind him and of men talking and laughing. When the riders came into view, he saw at once that they were grand people.

They were richly dressed and rode beautiful horses. Soon they were quite close. Adamnan hid behind the bushes at the edge of the track so as to let the horsemen pass. He did his best to keep the milk safe.

In spite of all his care, however, one of the horses brushed against him. He stumbled and fell. The jar rolled off his back and broke into pieces and all the milk was spilled. It was a terrible thing to happen, don't you think? What would you have done if it had happened to you? It is no use crying, you know. To make matters worse, the horsemen seemed to think the accident a great joke. They all laughed loudly, not caring one bit. The one who had knocked Adamnan down never even said he was sorry.

Adamnan was not in the least hurt, but he jumped up with such an angry look that the men laughed louder than ever. Then they rode away. Adamnan ran after them shouting, "That wasn't my jar. It was only lent to me. You'll have to get me another."

The men just rode on, not listening at all. Adamnan tore after them and he was so furious and disappointed that it made him run surprisingly fast.

"You'll have to get me some more milk," he yelled after them. "That was for poor scholars and they can't be left hungry just because of you."

The men rode on. By this time the laughing had stopped and they were talking of something else. Then the horsemen looked around and there was the little boy with the furious red face still at the tail of the last horse and still shouting at them. Never had they seen anyone run like that. It began to look as though they would never shake him off.

Now one at least of that company was a good man at heart, only somewhat careless as people sometimes are. He reined in his horse and said to the others, "Let's hear what the lad has to say." So all the men said, "Whoa," to their horses and stopped to listen to Adamnan.

He spoke up to them without fear, telling them that they were rude and bad to laugh at an accident so cruel to him. "You must get me another jar of milk to make up for the one you broke," he said, "because that jar had only been lent to me and I collected that milk, cupful by cupful, from many houses for the use of three poor students." Little Adamnan was quite stern.

One of those men on horseback was a very important person named Finnachta, who afterward became the High King of Ireland. When he heard Adamnan's story, he said the boy was right, that the accident was their fault and that the vessel of milk must be replaced. So the company of proud horsemen had to make a halt on their journey and one of them had to go back to the king's palace and bring in a chariot another jar of milk as good as the one that had been broken.

The whole affair made Finnachta interested in the way poor scholars had to live and while they waited he asked Adamnan many questions.

Later on, Finnachta brought to his own house those three older boys for whom Adamnan had been doing errands. And he never forgot the boy who had stood his ground so bravely and so well; he helped Adamnan, too, become a priest and they became great friends. When Finnachta was High King of Ireland and Adamnan the head of a great monastery of monks, they were able to help each other in a thousand ways.

damnan became a missionary and preached the Gospel in Scotland. He wrote many books about the life of those times which are precious to us now. He became Abbot of Iona, that lovely and holy island off the west coast of Scotland, and died there about twelve hundred years ago.

So that is the story of a little adventure happening to a boy which changed his whole life. Supposing he had just put up with the loss of the jar and milk and gone back to the hut, wailing and complaining?

Well, if he had there would have been no jar, no milk, no friendship with a king, and no story.

eath people are proud of their county, it is the the only one that is called *Royal,* the county of the High Kings of Ireland.

But kings are only kings and saints are saints; and Meath should be very proud of its saint, Benignus. He grew up in the district around Duleek where, nowadays, the best raspberries come from. Did you ever eat Duleek raspberries? Very nice mashed up with ice cream, I would say. But I had better get on with the story.

Duleek is on a pleasant little river called the Nanny. Men go to this river to catch brown trout; perhaps the boy Benignus fished for them, too — with a homemade rod and a worm for bait.

The River Nanny makes a grand boyhood companion: one can use it for paddling, floating boats, bathing, and fishing . . . and eat wild raspberries, frochans, and blackberries between whiles.

Benignus was the son of an Irish chieftain. The biggest event of his childhood — indeed, it proved to be the biggest event of his whole life — was the day St. Patrick came on a visit.

Of course the family had news of the great man's arrival and there were tremendous excitement and preparations. Benignus shared in the fuss: messages to friends and relations, moving things and getting things, buying things and borrowing things, fixing things and then unfixing them because they weren't quite right, people not knowing whether they were going or coming.

Do you know how it is? Has it ever happened in your family that an important visitor is expected and everyone starts doing everything at once?

Benignus helped in his small way and also asked a great many questions — far too many, his parents thought. Well, he learned that the main reason St. Patrick was coming was to baptize his whole family.

They were believers in Christ and they knew that the Message Patrick brought to Ireland was tremendously important and likely to change the whole nation (indeed it did as, thank God, you and I know well), but they had not yet been baptized. They were looking forward happily to this great Sacrament — the Opening of the Door Sacrament, one might call it.

They were the grown-ups; we don't know what was passing in young Benignus's mind.

Perhaps he was only hoping that the visitor would not be disappointing. So many of them are, you know. The grown-ups tell you that the person who is coming is wonderful and delightful and you believe them. He comes, he shakes hands with the grown-ups, talks a lot and laughs a lot; then he gets round to you, shakes your hand, too, but he doesn't seem to see you; he is child blind. The thing turns out to be a completely grown-up affair and your conclusion is that parents have very bad taste in "wonderful" and "delightful" people.

But this time there seemed to be hope. All the questions Benignus asked about St. Patrick got the right answers. For example, it came out that Patrick was brave and had had many exciting adventures. He had been put in prison twelve times for preaching about Christ.

Once, in prison, he had been chained to a wall. Once he had been sentenced to death, but the judges later changed their minds — perhaps they were afraid of the man who preached punishment for the wicked.

The most exciting story Benignus heard was this one: just as they were setting out, the driver said to Patrick, "You drive this time and I'll sit behind in your place."

Patrick was astonished; after all, the driver's job was to manage the horses. But he said nothing and did what he was asked to do — perhaps the driver was feeling sick or very tired.

When they were halfway on their journey, they had to go through a narrow road with high banks on each side. Patrick slowed the horse and was taking it carefully when a couple of men jumped up from behind the bank and threw a spear. It struck Patrick's driver who was sitting in Patrick's usual place. Then the men ran away.

When Patrick checked on his driver, he found that the man was dead. Then Patrick understood: his servant had given his life for him. The driver must have heard that an ambush had been prepared and purposely changed places so that Patrick would be spared.

Benignus was impatient to meet the man for whom another man would die.

He wasn't disappointing, this important visitor. He was great with children, and when he looked at them, he saw them.

After the greetings, St. Patrick baptized them all: father, mother, relations, friends, and Benignus. In fact, Benignus wasn't really Benignus at all until Patrick chose that special Christian name for him; he may have had a different name before that, but it doesn't matter in the least now.

After the ceremony, Patrick turned to the boy, praised the new clothes he had on for the great day and asked him questions, not silly questions that make a boy wiggle his toes — nothing about lessons and teachers — but good questions: How far can your boat sail? What size fish have you caught? Do you like raspberries better than blackberries, or blackberries better than raspberries? Real, sensible questions that a boy could answer straight out.

But they, the grown-ups, were restless; they didn't like to see Patrick talking so much to the boy. They moved off to the garden, edging the visitor along with them. For a time there was happy talk and then Patrick said that he was tired and would like to rest before he went on his journey. (The saint was always traveling up and down Ireland, preaching, baptizing, ordaining priests, and setting up places where Mass could be said.) They showed him a shady, quiet corner of the garden, saying that he would not be disturbed in that place. He lay down, covered himself with his cloak, and was soon fast asleep.

Benignus was surprised that a grown man could fall asleep like that in the daytime. But he understood why when he heard the others whispering together.

St. Patrick had traveled many miles that day, he had already preached three sermons and baptized hundreds of people, and anyway he never slept much at night because he prayed a lot at that time.

The people moved back to the house and left Benignus to watch over the sleeping visitor. Benignus stood staring, doing nothing for a while. He noticed that Patrick's sandals were white with the dust of roads, his clothes were all dusty, too, and there was even dust in his hair.

It was a hot summer day and the flies were a terrible nuisance; Benignus noticed them buzzing about the sleeping man. "Well, if a servant can die for Patrick," thought Benignus, "I can at least do one tiny thing for him." So he went off and picked some strongly scented plants — meadowsweet and water mint perhaps — and placed them all around Patrick, because flies don't like these strong-smelling plants.

"Stop!" It was one of the men from the house. "Don't do that! You'll wake him. Go away!"

Patrick did wake, but it wasn't Benignus's fault; it was the fault of the interfering man with the loud voice. Patrick rose up on his elbow. "Don't send him away," he said to the man. "He's a good boy. It may be that he will yet do wonderful things for the Church."

Once Patrick was awake, he thought he might as well stay awake. The others all came from the house and the happy talk went on again.

Someone told Patrick that Benignus could sing, so Patrick got him singing. After the usual clapping, Patrick said that he would very much like to have the boy singing everywhere he went, because such sweet singing would help people to pray better and raise their hearts to God during the Mass.

Then the time came for Patrick to go. His companions began to harness the horses to the chariots. The round of God-bless-yous and God-be-with-yous began.

Benignus stood looking on silently. He felt sad that the day was over, and he felt strangely lonely that Patrick, the man he had known only for a few hours, was leaving.

His mother noticed the boy's long face and she tried to comfort him. "Ireland is full of people wanting Patrick," she said. "We have to let him go."

Benignus did not think there was much consolation in that argument.

When at last all were starting off, Benignus did a surprising thing. He jumped into Patrick's chariot and rolled himself into a ball at the saint's feet.

His astonished parents shouted, "Benignus!" There was anger in their voices. All the other people groaned or made noises of vexation as if to say, "What are the children coming to these days?"

Someone tried to pull Benignus away, but he clung on as if he were glued. Then Patrick turned to the parents and said in a kindly way, "Perhaps you had better let him come with us. He wants to so greatly, and he will be safe with us."

For a second or two there was dead silence; everyone was shocked at Patrick's suggestion — could he possibly mean it?

Then they all talked at once: Benignus was too young. He had no sense. He wasn't nearly finished at school. Maybe in five years' time he could go. Maybe in two years' time. Maybe in one year. It was the parents and the relations who said those things. But there was another chorus, the followers of the saint: He's too young. He'll be in the way. Who will look after him? He'll be a nuisance.

But Patrick just smiled and said, "He'll be all right."

And so Benignus went with them, and he *was* all right, even though he never returned home again.

He sang in every church where the saint said Mass, and he learned how to teach, and how to preach, Christianity; later he became a priest himself and baptized people and did all the holy things a priest does.

Benignus was most useful to Patrick from the very beginning because, being born and raised in Ireland, he knew the country and the people and could put Patrick right when he was puzzled about things. You see, Patrick himself was not Irish, but Roman.

And to end the story, when Patrick was dying, he said that Benignus was the very best man in Ireland to be the next Archbishop of Armagh. The other bishops agreed and made Benignus head of the Irish Church.

I did say, didn't I, that the day St. Patrick came to visit was the biggest event in Benignus's life? That was certainly true.

here were a great number of Irish saints named Ciaran. The Ciaran I am telling you about this time was the first bishop of Duleek. I have already told you about St. Benignus of Duleek — it seems to have been a very good place for producing saints. Both Benignus and Ciaran lived in the same period as St. Patrick, away back in the fifth century.

When Ciaran became a priest he wanted to live alone in a solitary place so that he would get to know God by prayer, become a better priest, and so become better at bringing sinners to God. So he became a hermit. He built himself a little hut in the midst of the woods near the River Nanny — the same river on which the boy Benignus sailed boats and in which he used to fish. Ciaran meant to fish in it, too. He told himself he would eat fish and drink water — and that's all he wanted in this life. He would be free to pray every day for hours and hours.

The plan worked except that instead of being completely alone, he was soon surrounded by friends — animal friends.

Like many of the Irish saints, Ciaran had a strange power over animals; he had only to talk to them and they became tame. He loved them and they knew that he loved them and they didn't see any reason they should be afraid. But perhaps there was another reason, in this case, why the animals came to Ciaran's hut and made friends with him.

At that time, the country around the Nanny River was all covered with woods; there were no houses for miles and miles and, of course, no people. The wild animals were very curious about this strange creature who lived in a hut, fished in the river, and said so many prayers. They often came to peep at him.

The first that came was a deer with her fawn. Ciaran would find her outside his hut when he came out in the morning. She would quickly move away but, during the day, he would see her watching him with interest from a distance. Every day she got less timid and one day she came near enough for Ciaran to stroke her head. She liked that. The fawn saw that his mother was pleased and he went forward to have his head stroked too. Ciaran made a great fuss over the fawn and, of course, that was a great success with the mother. In a short while both doe and fawn were as tame and friendly as pet dogs.

Anybody who takes the trouble can tame deer — especially young deer — but it isn't everyone who can get them to work. Ciaran did. He trained the doe to pull logs for him to build a little church beside his hut. He even trained the fawn to pull logs also — small ones. Soon the three worked together: the man cutting down trees and sawing off the branches, the deer pulling the stuff to the place where the tiny church was going up. When Ciaran had the church finished, he said Mass in it; perhaps the deer stood outside watching quietly.

But before the church was built, Ciaran had collected other animal friends. One day as he worked, he saw a wild boar peeping at him out of the bushes.

He pretended not to notice, but he talked a great deal to the deer and it amused him to see that the boar was sort of jealous and wanted to be talked to also. This went on for several days until Ciaran turned to the boar and asked him straight out if he would like to live with them.

The boar was delighted, but not the deer. Indeed, the fawn ran under her mother when the boar came along and could not be persuaded to leave her. Deer and boars are not good friends and the less boars that deer see, the better pleased they are.

However, Ciaran persuaded them all to forget the past and live together in peace like Christians. After a time they agreed. Ciaran gave the boar a job working on the building too. He had a rule that anyone who joined him was to help with the work.

The next animal to come was a wolf. Ciaran had to give him an especially long talk about never, never doing anything to frighten the doe and her fawn. The wolf agreed, wagged his tail, and frisked all round Ciaran to show how glad he was to join the company. He, too, was given a job.

They liked the work, of course; you mustn't think that they were forced in any way: one of the happiest things in life is when people work together, each doing his share and all being happy and proud of the thing made, or built, when it is finished.

The next animal to come was a badger. He is a kindly animal and mostly sleeps during the day and roams about for food during the night. Ciaran didn't have to give the badger a long talk because he knew he was an easygoing, harmless fellow. The badger got night work to do, keeping guard for the others, bringing sticks for the fire, and things of that kind.

The last animal to join the band was a fox. Ciaran was very, very slow to take him in. Ciaran watched the fox for weeks and weeks, as it peeped round trees and wagged its tail at him, but Ciaran would only shake his head, or maybe pretend he didn't notice at all. However, one day Ciaran called the fox to come sit down beside him. First he patted the fox's head, then he gave one of his famous long talks.

"You know, I am sure," said Ciaran, "that you have a very bad reputation. Men say that you cannot be depended on and the other animals don't like you. Now, I'm not afraid of you, but I am anxious that you should bring no harm to the other animals here. We are a sort of a family, you know, and we want to stay like that, happy and peaceful. Will you try very hard to be good? Will you be so good that I will be glad, and not sorry, I allowed you to join us?"

The fox wagged his golden tail and his bright little eyes sparkled like diamonds. So Ciaran patted him again and said, "You are one of us now and you may join in the work we do."

They all lived together happily for quite a while: doe, fawn, boar, wolf, badger, and fox. Every morning they came to Ciaran and he told them the tasks they were to do for that day; they were gentle with one another and obedient to their master. Ciaran divided out his food with them and everything seemed happy and well.

ut one day, Ciaran missed his sandals. He had put them away because the weather had been warm, but the cold weather was coming on and when he went to look for them they were gone. He called the animals together and told them about his loss. No one seemed to know

anything about the sandals. Then Ciaran noticed that something besides the sandals was missing — the fox! He asked the others where the fox was. There was no answer.

"I'm afraid," he said sadly, "the fox has run off with my sandals." The other animals looked anxious and sad. But Ciaran was very upset indeed, not for the loss of the sandals (after all, he could get another pair) but that the fox had failed him. He often feared this might happen, but he had hoped and hoped for the best. Still, the worst had happened.

"Who'll find the fox for me?" he asked the others. The badger and the wolf both said they would. Ciaran selected the badger.

"You'd be the best," he said. "You know every inch of the country. Find him for me and bring him back, but don't do him any harm."

Off went the badger in his funny rolling way. He searched every fox covert for miles around and at long last found him.

The fox was lying down with the sandals beside him. He was just going to eat them when the badger flung himself on him and, growling fiercely, bit the fox's ears and tail.

The fox was so ashamed that he did not fight back. He just slunk into a corner of the den and stayed there. Then the badger took the sandals in his mouth and signed to the fox to follow.

Very slowly the fox came out, his head down, his tail down, looking the picture of misery. He followed the badger, but he hated doing it, and every now and again he felt like running away, never to return. Whenever, on that long journey back to Ciaran, the fox looked like running away, the badger dropped the sandals and pulled the fox's hair so that it hurt; then the fox would follow him again. At last both animals reached the hut and the badger proudly put the sandals down at Ciaran's feet.

For a long time the saint looked at the fox, saying nothing. And then he said, "I know you like the taste of sandals; it reminds you of the meat you ate before you joined us. But if you want to live with us, you must eat the things we eat, and above all you must not steal. Now, for your penance you must eat nothing for three whole days."

The fox did what he was told. He fasted for three days to show Ciaran and the other animals that he was really sorry for his bad deed.

When the three days were over, they were all happy again and the matter of the stolen sandals was put out of mind altogether.

I would like to end this story by saying that Ciaran and his animal friends lived happily ever after.

They didn't, though, because people soon discovered Ciaran's hideout in the woods and came to him to learn about God. Every month more and more people came to be taught and in the end the animals went back again to the woods, because they did not like to live where there were crowds.

And, indeed, I don't blame those animals for running away from crowds.

ellyfish, icebergs, and cold winds come into this story — perhaps you had better put on some extra clothes before you hear it. It is about a man named Cormac, one of Ireland's sailor saints, a great friend of St. Columcille, and a great man for doing the hard thing for our Lord's sake. He lived in the seventh century.

When Columcille was leaving Ireland (and sad he was to go, but that's another story), he left his good friend Cormac in charge of his monastery in Durrow. Columcille then went off to Scotland and the Scottish islands to preach Christ; and he set up a great monastery on the island of Iona.

One day, who should turn up there but Cormac — the person who should have been in the middle of Ireland minding an important monastery.

"What brings you here?" said Columcille, rather crossly.

"I have come to tell you," said Cormac, looking serious and determined, "that I have left Durrow forever and I put another man in my place to take charge."

"Left Durrow! What did you do that for?" Columcille loved Durrow and he loved Cormac and when he had made Cormac Abbot of Durrow, he thought he had done the best thing for God, Ireland, Durrow, and Cormac. He was very sad. All his grand plans had come to nothing.

Cormac explained. He said that it did not really suit him to be in charge of other men. It bothered him so much that he could not say his prayers. He wanted very much to be alone, or just with one or two companions. He wished he lived on a desert island where he could spend all his time praying and so get nearer and nearer to our Lord whom he loved. And now he planned to go far away over the sea in search of such an island.

Columcille, of course, thought this was a crazy idea and he did his best to persuade Cormac to go back to Ireland. How he had hated leaving Ireland himself! What tears he had shed! Columcille had to go to preach Christ's message, but Cormac was wanted in Durrow. Leave Ireland! Was there ever such a mad idea! "Death itself in Ireland," Columcille said very solemnly, "is better than life everlasting in another country."

But it was no good. Cormac had made up his mind; his heart was set on finding a remote island.

They said, "God be with you," to each other.

"Help me with your prayers," said Cormac.

"I will surely," replied Columcille. "It is all I can do for you now."

And Cormac and his two companions shoved their little boat off the sand and out into the rock-edged cove and then away — very, very slowly — over the wide sea.

All went well for a week or so; they took turns at the oars; the weather was fairly good. Cormac was very happy: he loved the sea and he hoped soon to be in a place where he could think about God and pray as he felt he ought to pray. The sea helped Cormac to pray. For some reason he could never pray on land.

All went well until a tremendous southerly gale arose. It blew for fourteen days and nights and they could do nothing except let themselves go with the wind. They saw themselves being driven hundreds of miles out of their course and being pushed on up to the icy North Pole as oars were no use against such strong wind. They were powerless. Then there was the anxiety about food; they had only a few weeks' provisions stored in their little boat, so they had to ration out the food and drinking water. A gale and food running short were bad enough, but there was worse to come.

Very soon the little helpless boat was driven into a region of towering icebergs and frozen seas: terrible cold, terrible silence, terrible darkness at night and not a hope in the world of a hot meal!

Suddenly they began to notice something — another terror. In the holes between the ice they saw horrible jellyfish. Jellyfish about the size of a hand are common but these were the size of a person's head — a big head at that. Jellyfish sting, even the hand-sized ones; these Arctic Sea jellyfish with the feelers as long as arms, stung much worse. Cormac and his companions soon found this out. You see, the oars kept getting entangled in the jellyfishes' feelers and the men would lean out of the boat to try to free them. First one, then another got stung and so bad was the sting that their arms were paralyzed. It was a real plague — a plague of jellyfishes!

They were so hungry and so cold, and there seemed to be no hope at all — no one to come to the rescue, no chance that the wind would change. So they prayed — they prayed as hard as anyone ever prayed before or since. Prayer goes a long way and very quickly: only God alone knows how far prayer can travel and how fast it can travel. We stupidly think that radio messages, telegrams, and telephone calls go fast and far, but we forget that prayer flies faster than lightning and goes so far that no man can understand how far.

hile Cormac was wedged between the ice and the jellyfish, Columcille was writing peacefully in his cell in the monastery at Iona. He wasn't thinking of Cormac in the least; his mind was full of very different things — perhaps he was making up a poem, perhaps he was writing a sermon. Suddenly Cormac flashed into his mind; Cormac, his friend, in danger, calling out for help!

Columcille didn't stop to think why Cormac came to his mind and how prayers go rushing around Heaven and earth until they are answered. No, he acted: he dropped his pen, ran to the chapel, and rang the bell loud and long.

The monks were all busy at their tasks: one was grinding corn, another was making bread in the bake house, another was spinning wool, another was mending sandals, and others were working in the field and garden. They all looked up in surprise when the bell clanged. This wasn't the hour for prayers. But they didn't waste time arguing; they downed tools and ran to the chapel.

"Why do you call, Holy Abbot, is there something wrong?"

"It's Cormac," explained Columcille. "He's in the most terrible danger. We must pray for him with all our might, or he's lost."

So the monks filed into the chapel, bowed their heads, and began praying with all their heart. I wonder what was happening in the places they left so hastily. Did the bread get burned? Was a horse left yoked to a cart and did it get into a tangle? Did the hens break into the corn? However, no one dared stop praying until Columcille gave the signal. When they looked at him they were delighted to see him smiling.

"What about Cormac now?" a young monk asked eagerly.

"He is safe," said Columcille. But he didn't look at the young monk; he was looking out to sea, to the long, long straight line under the sky. "He is safe, thank God. And what is more, he'll be here with us again in a few weeks' time."

At the exact moment the monks came out of the chapel in Iona, the wind changed for Cormac and his two men near the North Pole. The icebergs shifted and there was a clear expanse of water for rowing. And how they did row with the wind at their backs! Great joy was in their hearts to be leaving this horrible place and to be facing back for Scotland again.

It wasn't long before Cormac arrived in Iona — Columcille had spoken true. The monks gave the poor storm-tossed men a great welcome. Cormac rested for a while and probably had some huge breakfasts and dinners to make up for all the starvation among the icebergs. When he was strong, he told the story of his adventure to Adamnan, who wrote it down in a book, and so the story has come down to us.

Cormac was a great sailor but not so well known as Brendan. The reason is easy to tell: Brendan came back to Ireland after his many adventures and discoveries on the sea. He told his stories to his friends, and they told them to others. But Cormac never came back to Ireland. He died on some lone island far away and we have no other story except this one.

Good St. Cormac found the desert island he looked for and got close to God. That is all we know.

odomnoc was one of the many Irish saints who first had to go out of Ireland to learn how to be a priest. He was a student before the great Irish schools of Bangor and Clonard and Clonfert and Clonmacnoise came into being.

Modomnoc went in a sailing boat across the English Channel to the great monastic school in Wales that had for headmaster a saint named David.

All the pupils in David's school had to work as well as study. They helped in the fields, or in the garden, or at building. David's monastery was such a big, busy place that every pupil in it could find something to do pleasing to his taste.

Modomnoc was given charge of the bees, and he simply loved it. The monks were glad of this because, although nearly everyone likes honey very much, not everyone likes to take charge of the bees that make the honey.

But Modomnoc happened to like the bees almost more than their honey and that is saying quite a lot.

He was most successful with his bees. He kept them in straw beehives called skeps in a special sheltered corner of the monastery garden, and all around the hives he planted the kind of flowers that he knew bees love. Every time they swarmed, he captured the swarming bees very gently and lovingly and set up yet another hive. He talked to the bees as he worked among them and they buzzed around his head in clouds as if they were talking back to him. And, of course, they never, ever stung him.

At the end of the summer, they gave him loads and loads of honey. Modomnoc had to ask the other monks to help carry it all from the garden. The monks were never without this most pleasant addition to their meals. They were able to make lots of mead, too, which is a delicious drink made of honey. And David was very glad indeed that he had put Modomnoc in charge of the bees, because never before had they given such good results in that school.

The good Modomnoc thanked God for his success, and he also thanked the bees. He would walk among the skeps in the evening and talk to them, and the bees would crowd out to meet him.

All the other monks carefully avoided that corner of the garden, walking past it in a hurry, because they were always afraid of being stung.

As well as thanking them, Modomnoc worked very hard, too, for his bees. He saw that they were left plenty of honey in the winter to keep them well fed until the spring came again. He kept them warm and comfortable in their skeps. When a storm threatened, he tied down the skeps securely. When frost and snow came, he covered them up, so that his bees would not feel the cold too much.

ell, when Modomnoc's years of study were ended, the time came for him to return to Ireland and begin his work there as a priest. He was very happy, of course, at the thought of going home again, but he knew he would be lonely for his bees. He had made their little world into a happy place and he was sorry to leave it.

When, at last, the day of his departure came, he said good-bye to David and all the monks and to all his fellow students. Last of all, he went down the garden to say good-bye to his bees. They came out in hundreds of thousands in answer to his voice and never was there such buzzing and excitement among the rows and rows of hives.

The monks stood looking and listening from a safe distance and they wondered at the commotion. "You'd think the bees knew," they said. "You'd think they knew that Modomnoc was going away."

At last the Irishman tore himself away from the garden and walked resolutely down to the seashore, where the sailors were waiting with the boat that was to take them to Ireland. Modomnoc got into it, they ran up the sail and the journey homeward began.

When they were about three miles from the shore, Modomnoc saw what looked like a little black cloud in the sky in the direction of the Welsh coast. He watched it curiously and as it approached, he saw to his amazement that it was a swarm of bees that came nearer and nearer until finally it settled on the edge of the boat near him. It was a gigantic swarm — all the bees from all the hives, in fact. The bees had followed him!

This time Modomnoc did not praise his friends. "How foolish of you," he scolded them, "you do not belong to me but to David's monastery. How do you suppose the monks can do without honey, or mead? Go back at once, you foolish creatures!" But if the bees understood what he said, they did not obey him.

They settled down on the boat with a sleepy kind of murmur, and there they stayed. The sailors did not like their passengers in the very least. (You have to know bees to love them.) The sailors did not understand them and had no wish to.

They asked Modomnoc roughly what was to be done. He told them to turn the boat back for Wales. It was already too far for the bees to fly back, even if they wanted to obey him. He could not allow his little friends to suffer for their foolishness. But the wind was blowing the boat to Ireland and when they turned back, the sail was useless. The sailors had to furl it and row back to the Welsh coast. They did it with very bad grace, but they were too much afraid of the bees to do anything else.

David and the monks were very surprised to see Modomnoc coming back and looking rather ashamed. He told them what had happened. The moment the boat had touched land again, the bees had made straight for their hives and settled down contentedly again.

"Wait until tomorrow," advised the Abbot, "but don't say good-bye to the bees any more. They will be over the parting by then."

Next morning, the boat was again in readiness for Modomnoc and this time he left hurriedly without any fuss of farewell. But when they were about three miles from the shore, he was dismayed to see again the familiar little black cloud rising up over the Welsh coast.

This time he knew what it was. He was so overcome at the thought of the trouble he was giving to everyone that he had not the heart even to scold the bees. As for the sailors, they asked for no directions this time, but just turned the boat and made for the shore as fast as ever they could row the boat.

Once more the shamefaced Modomnoc had to seek out David and tell his story. "What am I to do?" he pleaded. "I must go home. The bees won't let me go without them. I can't deprive you of them. They are so useful in the monastery."

David laughed and said, "Modomnoc, I give you the bees. Take them with my blessing. I am sure they would not thrive without you anyhow. Take them. We'll get other bees later on for the monastery."

The Abbot went down to the boat and told the sailors the same story. "If the bees follow Modomnoc for the third time, take them to Ireland with him and my blessing." But it took a long time and a great deal of talking to make the sailors agree to this.

The sailors did not care who had the bees as long as they weren't in their boat. They explained to the Abbot that bees were just the very kind of passengers they never wanted. No, thank you. Let someone else take them to Ireland. If they caused trouble on the boat, why no one could sail it and they might all be drowned. "Anything but bees," they said. "Wild animals, yes, but bees, no."

The Abbot said that the bees were not likely to give much trouble with Modomnoc around, but the sailors asked why they had not obeyed Modomnoc when he told them to go back to the monastery. No, they didn't like it. Bees were bad enough but these bees, Modomnoc's bees . . . Well, their faces said plainly that they thought the bees were bewitched. But at long last they were persuaded to start again.

For the third time the boat set off for Ireland, Modomnoc praying hard that the bees would have sense and stay in their pleasant garden instead of risking their lives on the sea. But for the third time he saw what he dreaded, the little black cloud rising up in the distance, coming nearer and nearer until he saw it was the same swarm of bees again. It settled on the boat once more.

This time the boat did not turn back. Modomnoc coaxed his faithful friends into a sheltered corner, where they quietly remained during the whole journey, much to the sailors' relief.

When he landed in Ireland, Modomnoc set up a church at a place called Bremore, near Balbriggan, in County Dublin, and here he established the bees in a happy garden just like the one they left in Wales. The place is known to this day as "the Church of the Bee-keeper."

lannan belonged to the seventh century. He was a rich man's son; that is the first thing you must know about him. This made it much harder for him to be a saint.

He was the son of a king named Turlough. When Flannan was growing up, he had the very best food that could possibly be had; he wore the very finest clothes; and he had a great crowd of servants always around him to whom he had only to say, "Do this," or, "Do that," and the thing was done.

He learned to ride almost as soon as he could walk. He became a marvelously good rider, able to control the wildest horse and never falling off even at the very highest jump.

He loved riding and he loved to be praised and admired for his horsemanship. He was so good at it that he was allowed to follow the chase while still only a small boy and that was certainly the biggest thrill of his life. It meant riding fast through forests, or up mountain sides after wild boar or deer; jumping every obstacle that came in the way; never admitting he was tired even when the chase lasted the whole day long; bringing home on the saddle before him the prized trophy of the chase, the horns of the deer, perhaps, or the tusks of the boar; having a huge supper at the end of it with all the grown men, who clapped him on the back and drank his health.

It is not surprising that when Flannan was a boy he simply lived for the days when the king's household followed the chase.

The army, and the life of an army, were his next interest. He first had to learn how to shoot with a bow and arrow and, as his aim became true, his father kept getting him bigger bows and more deadly arrows such as the real soldiers had. Then he had to learn how to wear armor: first he wore a small helmet and a small shield and then big heavy ones. He had to learn how to fight with a spear, on foot and on horseback. Flannan found all this enormously interesting and he tried his very hardest to be good at all the crafts of a soldier. It was a very proud day for the boy when his father put him at the head of a company of soldiers and trusted him to lead them out to battle. Flannan was then a prince in fact as well as in name.

Then, quite suddenly, Flannan made up his mind to be a priest and give up forever the chase and the army.

It cannot have been easy for him because he knew his father was depending on him to succeed as king. Nevertheless, since his parents were good Christians, they gave in to him as soon as they saw he was really determined to lead a different life.

The thing Flannan found hardest to give up was power to rule. He did not mind so much giving up the good food or the fine clothes, but he did find it hard to give up his power as a prince. You know, it really is great fun to have a crowd of people always ready to do your slightest bidding; and it is still better fun for a boy to be the leader of soldiers and make fifty men act as one man at a single word of command.

When he began to study, he worked away at his books like the poorest boy in the monastic school. He also very cheerfully did the hard jobs that these students had to do, such as grinding corn with the handstone, fetching buckets of water, milking cows, washing up, and cleaning.

In time he finished his studies and became a priest. Then he went to Rome, where he stayed for a while, completing his education in the center of the Christian world.

It was a great enlightenment for Flannan to go to Rome: among other things, he saw stone churches there such as he had never seen in Ireland. He saw the interior of those stone-built churches decorated with mosaic pictures — another thing he had never seen at home. The Pope of that time, John IV, was the Pope who consecrated Flannan bishop. Then back went the new bishop to his native Clare and began building up a Christian life among his own people.

lannan's father helped him in setting up a monastery of his own, and among other gifts, he gave his son some beautiful cattle. There were many robbers going the roads of Ireland in those days and some of them soon set greedy eyes on the nice cattle they saw grazing in the monastery fields.

One night, the robbers stole a couple of cows and drove them far away to their hideout in the mountains, where they slaughtered them and hung them up in a cave. The robbers laughed very gleefully over this raid — it had been so easy. They said to one another, "Little by little, we'll take all Flannan's cattle, and we'll live easy and cheap for the winter!" It certainly looked easy — you see, when they stole things from a king or a chieftain, they were liable to be followed by soldiers and killed for their wickedness; but when they stole from the monks, it was different: they were never followed.

Some days later, the robbers went back to their hiding place in the mountains and prepared to make a great supper for themselves out of Flannan's beef.

First, they kindled a huge fire and hung over it a great iron pot which they filled with water. Then they cut up the beef into nice pieces and put it in the water with some salt. The fire soon blazed up and began to roar. The robbers were simply starving. They had had nothing to eat all day. They left one man in charge of the pot and the others arranged the camp while the supper was cooking. They groomed and watered their horses and collected bracken for beds for themselves for the night. Finally, they began to shout to one another:

"Here, is that meat ready? I'm dying of hunger!"

"So am I!"

"So am I!"

The man in charge of the pot shook his head at the others. He seemed to be puzzled. One of the gang ran over, lifted the lid and looked into what he expected was by this time a savory stew, but the water was still stone cold and the meat still raw.

"You great fool," he roared to the man in charge. "Can't you build a fire yet?"

"Fool yourself!" shouted the other, angrily. "Can't you see the good fire?"

"It's not going strong enough," said the first one. "You'd need kicking to make you work."

The other robbers began to gather round.

"Here, let me at it," said another, roughly. "There's not one of ye can make up a fire."

"I've done nothing but stand here and stoke that fire," grumbled the first man. "There's a cartload of wood gone under that pot already."

"Nonsense. It's asleep you were," said another.

So they quarreled and strove around the fire, hitting one another and even pulling out their knives to kill one another.

"I tell you," said the man who had been left in charge of the pot, as soon as he could make himself heard in the din, "I tell you there's some magic in this. This pot won't boil."

They wouldn't believe him. They flung logs on the fire until their arms ached from cutting and dragging them. Then they felt the water and again they looked at one another in amazement. It was still stone cold. They cursed the pot and raged at it. Finally they had to fill their empty stomachs with bread and herbs and water to stifle the pangs of hunger. Then they all began to talk again about the puzzle of the raw meat.

"It's because it's Flannan's meat," one robber said soberly.

"That pot would boil for Flannan," said another. "It's because we stole the meat from him."

No one spoke for a long time then. They were thinking hard.

At last the robber chief said, "That must be a great God the Christians have when He can protect His people without arrows or knives."

But they made one more try. They built a last great fire, up and all around the pot until it was nearly covered. Then they went to sleep. When they awoke in the daylight, there was still a good fire left, but the water in the pot was still cold, the meat still raw. There was nothing for it but to pile all the stolen meat on to a cart and bring it back to Flannan's monastery.

When they arrived, the Abbot received them with kindness and never even scolded them, though he could not help laughing when he heard their story.

They said they wanted to know about the Christians, so he taught all the robber gang the true religion. They gave up their wild life after that and never again killed anyone or stole anything.

have two little stories to tell you about St. Finbarr. They are about his childhood and happened long before he founded the city of Cork and became its first bishop. In the first story Finbarr is only seven; in the second, he is a schoolboy, but not that horrible person a "Model School Boy." I hope you will like this saint who wasn't too good to be true when young. I hope you will say an occasional prayer in his honor.

Finbarr was not the name he was christened; it was a pet name. When he was three or four years old, he had such wonderful long fair hair. Everyone — parents, uncles, aunts, neighbors — began calling him Finbarr, which in Irish means "Fair Crest" or "Fair Hair." The pet name stuck and became in time a saint's name which men today are proud to own.

When Finbarr was seven years old, three priests came to visit his mother. After a time, the boy was brought along in the usual way and the priests asked him the usual sort of puzzling questions. But one question was easily answered.

"Well, young man, what are you going to be when you grow up?"

"A priest," answered Finbarr, quick as a wink.

Of course the visitors were pleased after all, they were priests themselves. But his mother wasn't so pleased. "Oh yes," she said, "he's always saying that, but we don't take any notice. What would a child of seven know?"

But the priests were not put off by the mother. One of them turned again to Finbarr and said, "If you really mean that, you would have to leave your mother and your nice home and come away with us."

"I know that well," answered Finbarr, "and I am ready to come with you this minute."

So that was that. He went with them.

Of course his mother put in many cautions and told the priests the boy was very young and that twelve would be a more suitable age than seven, and that he probably would be lonely, and all the rest of it. But at last she agreed to Finbarr going away to learn to be a priest.

You see, in those days the Irish were filled with great love for Christ; they wanted everyone in the world to know how Christ died to save mankind; they wanted more and more priests to go out and preach the Gospel. I doubt very much if today three priests could call at a house and take a little boy away without arousing a great fuss.

They had a long way to go to the monastery where the priests lived. Finbarr stepped out bravely with the priests and their servant boy. For at least half the journey, Finbarr was good as any of them, taking man-sized steps and saying nothing. Then, all at once, he began to cry.

"What's the trouble? Are you lonely?" asked one of the priests.

Finbarr shook his head, but he went on weeping.

"Do you want to go back home?" There was disappointment in the speaker's voice.

Finbarr shook his head again. Then he did what is always so difficult to do when you are weeping — he managed to talk. "I'm thirsty," he said. Wasn't it a simple complaint?

The three priests were surprised; they were too grown-up to think of an ordinary thing like thirst. The boy wants a drink, where are we to find water? They looked around them helplessly. There didn't seem to be a well or stream within miles.

They asked Finbarr if he could last out until they got to the school and the poor child answered sadly that he would do his best. The fact was, however, that Finbarr was almost dying of thirst and the priests knew it.

The journey to the school brought them through a wild country where deer were plentiful. While they were talking, they saw a doe with her fawn looking down at them from a little hill.

One of the priests got an idea. "Go up there," he said to the servant boy, "and milk that doe."

It was a crazy order to give. Deer are wild; does strongly object to people coming near them at all, much more do they object to being treated just like cows and milked. The other priests looked amazed; the servant boy spluttered that deer are wild and that does don't stand still.

"Try anyway," said the priest.

So the servant took a bowl out of his pack and went up the hill. They all watched to see what would happen.

The doe stood perfectly still and when the young man stretched out his hand to stroke her, she licked it. Then she allowed him to take milk from her udder. It was extraordinary.

The boy came back with a bowl of lovely milk (deer's milk is said to be much nicer than cow's milk or even goat's milk) and Finbarr had his badly needed drink.

"It is a sign," said one of the priests quietly. "It is a sign from God that Finbarr is to be a priest."

He was right. Finbarr was to be a great priest and to be highly favored by God.

hen the boy was nine or ten years old, he was sitting in the schoolhouse one day, learning his lessons with the other boys. It was wintertime and it began to snow. Now, snow is rare in County Cork and when it comes there is great excitement; even at the present time Cork people think snow a sort of a treat. So little Finbarr was thrilled at the novel sight: feathery flakes dancing about, everything getting whiter and whiter.

It was the first snow he had ever seen and he found it hard to go on with his lessons. He got out for a moment and saw that the thatched roof of their little round schoolhouse was capped with white. It was a marvelous sight. Then he went back to his books, but he could not do his lessons at all. He was dying to go out and play in the snowy fairyland.

After a time he asked the teacher if he might go out again. He badly wanted another good look at the snow-hooded thatch.

"Finish that lesson and then I'll give you an hour off to play," said the teacher. Finbarr glanced at the lesson; it would take at least an hour to finish it and by that time it would be dark outside. Finbarr thought his teacher pretty mean not to let him have another look, but he said nothing. He worked away or worked away with one part of his mind and with the other part he prayed that the snow would last and that the daylight would last and above all that the funny snow cap on top of the school would last.

The snow stopped and darkness came on. The teacher put a rush light on the table and the boys went on with their long lesson. But there was a chance yet. Finbarr stopped his lesson to pray with all his heart and mind that the snow wouldn't melt before he was free from lessons. But it seemed that the prayer was no use: by the time the lesson was finished it was pitch dark and as the boys went to the house where they slept, they could see nothing.

Then the thaw began. When Finbarr was dropping off to sleep that night he could hear the plop-plop of snow falling off trees. He felt very sad. It was all going, the lovely white covering on trees and fields and roofs all going and he had had only one tiny look at it.

Next morning when he got up, the sun was shining and all the snow had melted. It was over; there was nothing to hope for. But as the boy walked to the schoolhouse, he could hardly believe his eyes, for there was the snow on the thatched roof just as it had been the day before!

The teacher wasn't as mean as Finbarr thought and told the boys that they could have an hour's play as had been promised them the day before. Finbarr did not join in the games but spent his time admiring the snow on the roof. It was a lovely sight: roundy, smooth, glittering and winking in the sunshine. He could reach up to the snow, too, and feel it, and make lumps and balls with it. He was very happy.

Only Finbarr noticed the snowcap on the schoolhouse; everyone else was too busy that day, or else they were the sort of people who never notice anything. But the snow lasted on the thatched roof for several days, though it had melted everywhere else. Then everyone — boys and masters — certainly did take notice. How could this be? How could snow stay in one place and go from every other place? They also noticed that Finbarr seemed to be extra happy about the event and they questioned him. They found out how he especially prayed that it might last and how he longed to have a good look at and handle this beautiful gift from God. And God had smiled at the boy and granted the boyish thing that he asked.

It was a sign (they said) that Finbarr was going to do great things. The Abbot ordered that the story be written down in the monastery book so that it would be remembered always.

It is now more than thirteen hundred years since Finbarr was a schoolboy praying that the snow might last a little while longer. Much snow has fallen since then, and all of it is melted and forgotten, all except Finbarr's special snowfall.

here are truly a great many St. Colmans in Ireland. Once I counted nine different ones, but then someone told me that there are many more than that, so I gave up trying to get the complete list. Anyhow, this Colman that I am telling you about now is called Colman-Elo, to mark him out from the other Colmans.

Colman-Elo was a monk and a great teacher. The story I am going to tell you is about what happened to one of his pupils and how Colman's prayer for him was answered.

The little boy's name was Baithin (pronounced 'baw heen') and there were always two things said about him in school: one, that nothing, absolutely nothing, would stay in his head, and two, that he remembered nothing that was ever done against him, meaning of course that he never sulked. Now you know exactly the kind of boy Baithin was.

It is very nice to have a boy with a sunny tempera-
ment who never sulks, but the other thing, that nothing would stay in his head, was certainly troublesome.

When Baithin was nine or ten, Colman, his
teacher, made up his mind that things would really
have to be *made* to stay in his head. First he warned
Baithin several times that he would have to try harder.

One day, when there had been was no improve-
ment, he punished Baithin because he was not even
trying to learn. The boy was annoyed at being punished and ran out of the school.

Colman ran after him to bring him back. But the
boy could run much faster than the teacher and when
they came to a thick wood, Baithin darted into it.
Colman gave it up then and turned sadly home. It is
quite useless to try to catch anyone in a wood. A boy
could hide there forever among the thick trees.

When Colman got back to the monastery, he
went straight to the chapel. There he prayed that
Baithin would be safe, and that he would come back
again soon and stick to his lessons like a good boy.

t first Baithin was simply delighted at
his own cleverness in escaping. He
felt proud that he could run so much
faster than Colman.

It was a sunny day. The birds were
singing. There were the most lovely

fresh scents in the wood. He said to himself, "Huh, this is better than the old lessons. I cannot learn anyhow. They all say that nothing will ever stay in my head. So I will never go back to school again. I am free now for ever and ever."

He strolled along, whistling merrily, and presently he came to an open space in the wood. Here he met a man with a bundle of stakes on his back. The man threw his bundle on the ground, picked out one of the stakes with care and thrust it deep into the earth. Baithin watched him curiously and then said, "What are you doing?"

"Building a house," the man told him.

"What," cried Baithin, "building a house with one stick! How silly! You'll never do it."

"Oh, yes," said the man, "I can and I will. If you stay here with me, you'll see me do it."

So Baithin, laughing because he did not believe the man, sat down on the ground and watched him.

He was very glad to have a rest anyway.

Now, let me tell you how they built houses in those far-off days. First a circle of stakes was made; then more stakes, or wattles, were woven across through the standing ones. This made a wall, which was later plastered over with clay that dried quickly. Then a thatched roof was put on.

A man could sleep in this and be snug and warm. We build our houses in a different way today, with cement blocks or brick, but still you must remember that the grandest and finest house is begun with just one brick or just one block.

Well, the man put another stake in the ground beside the first one, about a foot away from it, then another, then another, until he had made a complete circle of stakes, with a space left for a door. He was glad of the boy's company and, as he worked, he went on talking.

"Fair and easy, you know. Little by little. Nothing is done in a hurry. Bit by bit it goes. Watch now and you'll see."

Baithin watched the man long enough to see that he really was making a house from that very small beginning of one stick. And the thought came into his head, "If I had stuck to my lessons like that, very slow at the beginning and little by little, perhaps I, too, would have been able to learn."

his thought was not a welcome one, for, after all, Baithin had made up his mind never to go back to school.

So he jumped up and continued on his way to find something more interesting.

All at once the sun went behind a cloud and it began to rain. The boy ran under an oak tree to take shelter. He leaned against the trunk and looked up at the green, leafy roof over him. Then he noticed that there was just one opening in the leaves where a heavy drop kept coming through on to the ground.

For want of something better to do, he dug his heel into the ground and made a hole under the drop, quite a good, deep, round hole to contain the water. Then he leaned against the tree again and watched. The water dripped into it, drip drop, drip drop, steadily like that, for it was a long heavy shower.

Baithin kept on staring down until the hole was quite filled with rain. By the time the sun shone out again, what had been dry earth was now a little pool of water. And the thought came into the boy's mind, "Learning is a bit like that, drop by drop and little by little. Perhaps if I had kept trying to learn like that, I would know my lessons now."

The sun was shining again, but somehow Baithin did not feel so happy. He was getting hungry. Now, if Colman was a stern teacher, he saw that his boys were well fed. Baithin remembered that, too. All at once he made up his mind to go back to Colman and tell him his thoughts. You see, he had suddenly made up his mind he would try to get at learning in a different way: slowly and little by little.

It was a hard thing to go back, because feeling free really had been wonderful while it lasted. He returned the road he had come and to keep his courage up, he kept saying to himself, "However hard

I may find it, I will do it. However hard I may find it, I will do it."

When Baithin got to the school, he could not find Colman, because the saint was still praying for him in the chapel.

You see, it is not pleasant for a teacher to have to tell parents that their son has run away. Colman did not want to have to do that. Also he did not want anything horrible to happen to the boy. He just went on praying until he got the answer he wanted and saw Baithin walking in quite safe, saying that he was sorry and would like to talk with him!

Colman said he had better have his dinner first and then they could talk. Once Baithin had eaten a good dinner, he told Colman all his adventures in the wood and the thoughts that had come to him there.

And Colman thought it such a good story, he wrote it down, just as the boy told him, so that Irish boys might remember it always. He thought it might be helpful to them to learn their lessons Baithin's way, very slowly, with a small beginning, little by little.

I need hardly tell you that Baithin was never again punished for not learning his lessons. Afterward, whenever he got impatient thinking the lessons too long, too hard, too altogether horrid, he remembered the single stick that had grown into a house or the single drop of water that had grown into a pool, and this made him patient.

Baithin became a priest like Colman, able not only to read books but to write them, too. He became quite as great as his master.

St. Colman-Elo had many wise sayings, which were treasured in his own country for hundreds of years after his death. Did you ever hear this one: "What are the three things that are strongest under the sun?" Colman's answer was, "The Church, fire, water."

Irish children often see fire on the bog in early spring when men are clearing the spreading grounds, and they know what a terrifying sight it is when it becomes a living wall of flame that no man can quench. Colman-Elo said that the Church was like that: no man could overcome it.

And when he saw the river in flood, uprooting trees and carrying away bridges, he said the same thing, "See the strength of that water; the Church is like that."

his is a story about the patron saint of Kilkenny, who gave it its name: St. Canice, or Kenny.

My story is about such a tiny thing, such a very little thing, that I am almost afraid you will find it silly. It is all about the letter *O*.

There was once a great Italian painter named Giotto. The Pope at that time wanted someone to paint pictures on the walls of his palace and a friend who always advised him in such matters told him that Giotto was the best man in Italy to do the work. So the Pope sent a message to the artist, asking to see some examples of his work.

Giotto took a sheet of paper and just painted the letter *O* on it with one single sweep of his brush, an absolutely perfect circle. It was the only answer he sent the Pope.

The Pope laughed at this message, but he was quite satisfied and gave Giotto the work, because any artist who could do an *O* like that with just one turn of the wrist really could draw. So now *Giotto's O* has become a sort of saying among the Italians, who still talk and laugh about it.

But we have a greater man than Giotto in Ireland in the person of St. Canice, since he taught more with a bad letter *O* than Giotto did with his good *O*. I will tell you how.

Canice was sent to school in Britain when he was thirteen. The pupils in this school divided their time between learning lessons and working in the fields. It was a monastic school, of course. The chief thing the pupils learned there was how to be good Christians and many of them became priests.

Well, Canice had to do writing lessons, among other things. Our writing nowadays is plain, without decoration, but in the sixth century, when Canice lived, it was very beautiful. Every letter had to be lovely, but the capital letters were like pictures, with patterns around them, done in different colors, and little drawings set into them.

If you ever come to Dublin you should look at the Book of Kells in Trinity College to get an idea of what writing was like in those days. You could imagine that it would take a person about an hour to write one word in it, and perhaps you would be right, too.

Canice was a very good writer, and he loved the art of penmanship, as they called writing in those days. On this particular day, in the middle of his writing lesson, the bell rang. Canice dropped his pen right in the middle of the letter *O* and joined all the other boys going out to the fields to work.

Later on, however, when the teacher saw Canice's copy, he was not pleased. He called Canice to him and said, "Look at this. Isn't it a bad *O*?"

"Yes, very," admitted Canice, "but it isn't finished. When I finish it, it will be a good *O*."

"It will never be as good an *O* as if you had finished it in one round," said the master.

"I know that," said Canice.

"Well, why didn't you finish it?"

"Because the bell rang."

"The bell rang, did it?" said the teacher. "And are you so fond of field work that you couldn't even finish the *O* when the bell rang?"

Canice remained silent.

"Answer me," said the teacher.

"I don't like field work," said Canice. "I hate it. That is why I dropped my pen in the middle of the letter *O* when the bell rang."

"Hmmm," said the teacher, still not understanding, or perhaps pretending that he could not understand. And then he said to Canice, "But didn't you come here to learn how to write beautifully? You will never learn how to write if you make an ugly *O* that could be mistaken for a *U*."

"Yes," said Canice, "it is true that I came here to learn how to write well. But I also came to learn obedience and it is much, much harder to learn to be obedient than to learn to write well. I am taking the hardest thing first. That is why I dropped my pen in the middle of the letter O. I love writing so much that I would write all day if I had my wish. I hate to be disturbed at it."

"Well," said the teacher, "finish your copy now, and try not to let the join show in the middle of the letter O."

Later, when the teacher thought about this conversation, he knew that Canice was perfectly right, and that the boy of thirteen had really discovered one of God's secrets.

He told the other teachers in the school and one of them wrote down the whole story, but they never said anything to Canice at the time. Later on, when he became a bishop, and especially after his holy death, the story was told.

You see, before Canice came along, these monks used to think that a lesser kind of obedience would do. They thought it enough to come when you are called, even if you gave a big puff of a sigh, "Oh, dear," like that, to show what an effort it was to obey. But they quickly saw that Canice's sort of obedience was the best, that kind that is as quick as a flash and gives no sigh.

In due time the story went the round of all the other schools in Britain. From there it traveled to the schools in Scotland and back again to Ireland.

Canice's O soon became a proverb: "*O* for obedience." Anyone trying to learn this difficult business was told all about *Canice's O* and then he knew just what was expected of him.

Isn't it a simple little tale to make into a sort of headline for the great schools, a kind of watchword for the hardest thing to be learned there? But so it was for six hundred years, until those schools ceased to be. I think this story about a bad letter *O* is better than the one about the good *O*. Don't you agree?

Canice's feast is kept on the eleventh of October. Will you remember it and make use of it by praying to him on that day? You will find Canice a great friend because he really understood the difficulties that children have.

There are two kinds of children especially who should remember him: those who have to do writing lessons in school and those who find obedience hard. When you come to think of it, that seems to be all the children in the world.

 am glad to announce that this story will contain wolves, robbers, and a fierce bear.

Of course if you are one of those nervous children who look under your bed every night to see that there are no wolves or burglars hiding there, then you had better skip this story.

But I'll be disappointed; I'd like you to hear this tale of adventure; if it *does* give you frightening thoughts, I expect the only thing for you to do is to bring a big stick up to your bedroom tonight and be prepared for the imaginary bear, wolves, and robbers.

The adventure I am going to tell you about happened to St. Columbanus, who lived in the seventh century — that is fourteen hundred years ago.

It took place when he went to France. (It wasn't called France then, nor was it exactly the same country, but that doesn't matter.) Columbanus and his companions had already been given a good house by the king of those parts because he was so pleased that Irish men had come to preach the good news of Christ. The house was really an old castle; it was in bad repair and the monks set about fixing it up for themselves.

ne day Columbanus left his companions hammering away in the old castle and set off on a walk by himself in the direction of the forest.

He carried a book in his satchel (much the same thing as a schoolbag) and he was looking for a nice quiet place for a rest and a read. The book was the Gospel, the Book that set all things going: Irishmen traveling the long way to France, kings giving presents of castles, monks hammering at walls.

To re-read the Gospel always gave Columbanus great happiness; it made him feel that all the work and all the hardships were worthwhile. Above all, it made him feel that he must go on with the difficult business of making the pagans into Christians. The pagans in this country were very bad — very "tough" if you like to put it that way — and they nearly broke poor Columbanus's heart. He used often to say that he would rather have to deal with wild animals than with sinners. On this day, he certainly had to deal with wild animals as well as sinners.

He hadn't gone very far into the forest before a pack of wolves suddenly dashed out of a clearing and rushed upon him. There were about twenty of them, their tongues hanging out, red lights in their eyes.

Columbanus did nothing; he couldn't think of anything to do. Perhaps he didn't have time to climb a tree or perhaps all the trees had high branches and were not good climbing trees. He *did* nothing, but he *said* something, "O Lord, make haste to help me!"

The wolves made a ring around him. They sniffed greedily at his feet and some of them bit and closed their jaws on his cloak. It looked as if they would tear him to pieces any minute.

"O Lord, make haste to help me! O Lord, make haste to help me!" Columbanus continued to pray. The prayer held them off. If Columbanus had given one sign of fear, he would have been lost. They say that animals always know when you are afraid of them and that they will probably attack you if you are. To be fearless is a sort of a weapon in itself. At any rate, after a short time the wolves raced away without doing Columbanus the least harm.

e thanked God from the bottom of his heart; but as he continued his walk and his search for a nice quiet place to read, he heard men's voices — angry men — shouting and arguing among

themselves. He was frightened. The men were surely robbers and bad ones at that.

Then he saw them: hairy faces, wild eyes and knives stuck in their belts. They were the desperate sort, the ones who would think nothing of killing a man, especially if they met a stranger in the forest and the murder would never be found out by the king's soldiers. Columbanus got behind a tree. Along came the fierce robbers.

"I saw a fellow hiding behind one of those trees; I'm sure I did," said one rough robber.

"Did you?" The voice sounded pleased. "Maybe his purse would be worth cutting, or his throat, at any rate."

They darted toward the tree and went all around it. But they never saw Columbanus. The Good Lord had made haste to help him this time also, and Columbanus was invisible to the robbers.

"What sort of an idiot are you? You never saw anyone." The voice was angry.

"I did, I tell you!" And that voice was even more angry.

"You're a liar."

"And you're a fool."

So they went on calling each other terrible names and growling at each other like savage dogs. The other robbers sniggered and enjoyed the row. Soon they all went off.

"Well," thought the monk, "that was an even closer escape than from the wolves."

He went on quite a long way in the forest then, still looking for a peaceful place for a read. He came to a nice little cave in a clearing, near a lovely waterfall.

"This is the sort of place I'm looking for," thought Columbanus. "Maybe I'll stay here a few days: here is water to drink, a cave to sleep in at night or to shelter in if it rains, and a nice stone to sit on and read my book."

It was a great find. He went to the opening of the pleasant cave and looked in. He looked in; something with very fierce eyes looked out.

It was a bear, a she-bear with a cub. But this time, Columbanus was not afraid. He talked softly to the bear, just as if he was talking to a cat. And out of the cave she came, with her little fuzzy cub following. Columbanus stroked the mother's head and smiled kindly at the cub and it worked — the she-bear, the cub, and Columbanus became the greatest of friends.

Softness, kindness, and smiles often go a very long way and, another thing, animals are not always as savage as their growls would lead you to think.

Having made friends with the bears, Columbanus calmly took possession of their cave.

He cleaned it up for himself and put in a nice bed of dry ferns. Then he sat on the stone at the doorway and read his book. The bear and her cub sat quietly at the other side of the clearing and watched the monk with great interest.

If God had given those bears souls, they would probably have made very good Christians; they had the meekness of Christians. As long as Columbanus remained in the forest, the bears let him live in their cave in fact, they seemed happy to have him with them.

That is the end of the story as far as Columbanus's attempt to find a quiet place in the forest is concerned. But it is not the end of Columbanus's gentle way with animals. He had another adventure with a bear before he returned to the old castle where his friends were hammering away.

One day he came upon a dead stag some little distance from the cave. It had not been killed by hunters, but it had cut itself badly by running against a sharp stump of a fallen tree and had probably bled to death.

Columbanus was looking down at the dead beast and feeling sorry, because a stag is a noble animal and very beautiful, too, with its great horns. Suddenly he thought of something: sandals! Now, the skin or hide of deer makes a very good leather and good leather makes good sandals and the monks back at the castle had very old, bad sandals, or no sandals at all.

"If I mark the spot well, I can go back to the monks and tell them. They will bring out a cart and we will get the dead stag home and soon we will have leather and new sandals." Columbanus had hardly finished thinking this when he saw a bear.

The bear padded up to the dead stag, sniffed it with interest and began to lick the blood. It took no notice of Columbanus and Columbanus (being pretty used to bears by now) stood his ground. He did more: he walked over to the bear and told it severely to go away. But he gave his reasons also, "I found the stag first and I need it for sandals for the monks." Without so much as another lick, the bear drooped its head sadly and padded back into the depths of the forest from which it had come. To make matters better, the bear must have warned off all other wild animals because nothing touched the dead stag.

When Columbanus came back with the cart, he found the stag just as he had left it. The monks were very pleased and proud of their new sandals.

Columbanus made friends of wild animals, big and small. When he was kneeling at his prayers, the squirrels came around him and, for fun, would hide in the folds of his habit. After his prayers, he would play with them. Then the birds, seeming jealous of the squirrels, would fly down to be petted by him also. Columbanus was never lonely wherever there were animals or birds.

f I wanted fancy names for my stories of Irish saints, this one could be called "The Boy Who Laughed at His Father." Now, boys are supposed to respect their fathers, not laugh at them, but the boy in my story had every reason to laugh and, as it happened, the father was glad to be laughed at just this once. But I had better tell you the story straight before I begin to tell it mixed.

The boy was Laurence O'Toole, who became Archbishop of Dublin, and afterward St. Laurence O'Toole. He was Irish of the Irish: his mother's name was O'Byrne, which is a great old name like O'Toole itself. As for the Christian name, Laurence, you may use the Irish form of it if you like: Lorcan. I think Lorcan is a lovely name for a boy, one of the many lovely saints' names we have in Ireland.

When Lorcan was a little boy, he always heard his father and mother talking about the king of Leinster, whose name was Dermot MacMurrough. When they were talking of him, they looked troubled, as if this Dermot was a bad lot.

Well, if you know your Irish history, you will know that he was a bad lot. He was a troublemaker and a bully. As Laurence grew older, he began to understand.

(Dermot MacMurrough was afterward the cause of Ireland's woes. It was he who induced King Henry of England to come and take "possession of Ireland." It was said that he was against all men and all men were against him. Laurence's parents had every reason to worry about Dermot.)

Now Laurence's father was a prince as well; and although he was not as powerful a prince as Dermot MacMurrough, he still had many soldiers and servants, and he was rich in land and cattle.

Nonetheless Dermot was his overlord, and when Dermot went to war (he was fond of war), he would send word to Maurice O'Toole to come along and fight. Naturally, Maurice disliked fighting for a man he disliked and in a cause that he hated.

When his father came home, Laurence used to see him talking to his mother, looking very angry, shrugging his shoulders and making faces. It was just about a thousand times worse than watching our own Father tell Mother all about "The Boss" and what he said and what he did and how unreasonable he was.

One day, when Laurence was nine years old, his father came to him. He had a dark, worried look. Laurence knew at once that there was bad news.

"You'll have to go to Dermot MacMurrough's house and stay there for a while."

It was startling news and bad news. But the boy was the son of a soldier and not one to cry or make a fuss. He only said one word, "Why?"

"Because," said his father, "Dermot MacMurrough has just sent me a letter telling me that I must give him one of my sons as a kind of pledge that I won't rebel against his rule. I have to obey him. If I don't send you, or one of your brothers, he will send an army stronger than any army I could raise and just take you by force. If I don't send you, then he will come and take you." Poor Maurice O'Toole was extremely distressed. He was in a bad fix.

Now Laurence was the youngest of a big family; he had three older brothers and some sisters also. He thought of his big brothers and seemed to see a way out of his predicament.

"Why me?" he asked. "Why can't one of my brothers go to Dermot MacMurrough?"

"Because," said his father, "they are old enough to help me now and I need their help." (Perhaps he really meant "fight," not "help" — he looked as if he meant "fight" at any rate.) "You had better go. I can spare you more easily."

So it was sadly decided that Laurence should go. His mother tried to cheer him up and tried to get him interested in the clothes and things he would take with him, but his heart was terribly heavy. It was even heavy when they told him that Dermot was not unpleasant to live with, though he was a bad king.

There was only one ray of light: his mother said that she would try to get him home as soon as ever it was possible. Laurence squared his shoulders and rode away with one of his father's servants to Dermot MacMurrough's castle.

At first it was just as his mother had said it would be. The king wasn't often seen but when he was, he was nice and smiling. The castle was far grander than the O'Toole one; the food was good and everyone was kind.

Then there was a change. One day a servant came to Laurence and said, "Get your cloak. We are going on a journey."

"Is it far?" asked the boy.

"Yes, very far. Say no more but hurry up."

"What must I take with me?"

"Take nothing," said the servant.

When the two were riding along together, the servant became a little more friendly. He told Laurence that his father had not obeyed the king of Leinster and as a result the boy must suffer. To punish Maurice O'Toole, the boy was to be kept in prison:

not a prison of walls and iron bars, but a prison of mountains and bogs.

They rode a day from the king's castle and then they came to a lonesome place — no houses, no people, no fields, or gardens. The end of the journey was a miserable hut, half broken down and the rain coming in the roof. Here Laurence had to sleep and here he had to live as best he could.

By the king's orders, he got barely enough food to keep him alive: only bread, green stuff, and water. I need hardly say that his clothes soon became raggedy and that he had no means of mending them. As for lessons, well, he had no one to teach him and nothing to do all day — a dreadful thing to happen to a child. He was ten years old when he was sent away by the king.

Months passed. Laurence's parents did not know where he was; they barely hoped that he was alive at all. Then a year went by. He lost count of time and could not say how long he had been in the hut, without seeing any face except that of the man whose job it was to prevent him escaping.

Poor boy, he got pale and thin and was mother-sick, father-sick, and homesick all at the same time. Often he thought how lucky his brothers and sisters were to be cared for and at home.

He used to wonder if they thought he was dead. Why didn't Mother do something to help him? Hadn't she said that she would get him back soon? Why didn't Father come with his soldiers? But his family could do nothing because they did not know where their little Lorcan was; the cruel king of Leinster took delight in keeping that a secret.

ne day, when Laurence was twelve years old, he saw two men come riding up to the hut. The servant went out to speak to them.

After a great deal of talking, the servant returned with a letter. It was from the king and it said that the boy was to be handed over to these men. So one of them — a priest — took Laurence on his horse and off they went.

"Where now?" asked Laurence. He was weak and sick. He could hardly sit straight on the horse, and he had very little hope that he was going to be brought to a nice place.

"To the Abbey of Glendalough," said the priest cheerfully. "It's a grand place and it's not far. We'll be there soon."

"What's going to happen when we get there?" asked Laurence, still very sad in himself.

"A grand dinner to begin with," said the priest. And he and the other man began a joking conversation about roast chicken, bacon, apples, and cream.

"And after that?" asked poor Laurence.

"A bath," said the smiling priest, "and a haircut and good new clothes, so that you'll look again like the son of a prince."

"And Dermot MacMurrough?" asked the boy, hoping and hoping that it wasn't all a dream.

"You'll see no more of him," said the priest. "Your father is coming to the Abbey in a day or two to take you home."

It wasn't a dream. All happened as the priest had said: the clothes, the haircut, the bath, and even the apples and cream.

Soon Laurence began to feel well and happy again. He thought the Abbey a lovely place (certainly it is still to this day one of the most beautiful places in the world). He liked the boys there also; they were going on to be priests and such boys (it always seems to me) are extra jolly and up to tricks.

"Do you know," he said to the Abbot the second day he was in Glendalough, "I don't really want to go home at all. I like this place so much that I would like to go to school here and maybe be a priest like the other boys."

"Be a priest!" said the Abbot in surprise.

"Yes, I want to tell you that I made up my mind about that when I was in the hut. I do want to be a priest."

The Abbot said nothing to that. He was wondering how Maurice O'Toole would take the news.

With a great clatter and fuss, Maurice O'Toole came riding into the Abbey, twelve or fifteen horsemen attending him. He called for Laurence, hugged him tight, and said he didn't look too bad, and then that he wanted to talk seriously with the Abbot.

"On my way here," he said to Laurence and the Abbot, "I made up my mind that in thanksgiving to God for getting my son back safe and sound, I would give one of my sons to the Church."

Maurice looked important and he talked slowly as he continued, "There is one trouble: I cannot decide which son it should be. So I am going to put their four names in a hat and the name that you, Reverend Abbot, draw out will be a priest. He'll have to be a priest; he'll have to obey me." He sounded pretty fierce as he finished.

The Abbot glanced at Laurence and Laurence glanced at the Abbot. Then suddenly the boy threw back his head and laughed.

It was the first time Laurence had laughed in two years, so he made it a long, loud laugh, and that laugh got longer and louder when he saw the look on his father's astonished face which seemed to say, "What's all this about?" and "Young Man, how dare you laugh at me like that!" and so on.

At last Laurence brought his grand laugh to a stop. "Father," he said, "you needn't worry about making one of your sons a priest. And you needn't put names in a hat to do it — indeed and indeed, you needn't. *I* want to be a priest and, please God, I'll be one."

One hopes that even stern Maurice O'Toole laughed a little himself on hearing that good news.

his is a story about a very holy man named Blessed Thaddeus MacCarthy. He has not yet been made a saint but, as you probably know, to be called "Blessed" means that the Church considers the person worthy of becoming a saint.

Blessed Thaddeus should be of special interest to all boys with the name of Tighe or Tadhg or Thady — he is your saint. Of course if your surname is MacCarthy — a great and numerous clan in Ireland, especially in Cork and Kerry — then you may claim Blessed Thaddeus as a great and holy member of your family.

Blessed Thaddeus' feast day falls on October 25th; it was the day he entered Heaven. But I must begin my story at the beginning, not at the very end.

You know how short October evenings are?

The sun slips off to bed when you are having your tea; in fact, you're lucky if the lamps are not lighted before you finish. Then you run out again and you're disappointed to find it already dark. The evening is gone. You will hear people say rather sadly that "the days are drawing in." October evenings are the same everywhere. Far away in North Italy on the October evening I am telling you about, the day was rapidly drawing in.

A man was walking along the mountainous country road that leads from the city of Ivrea and goes toward Aosta. He was dressed as a pilgrim. In those days, when a person wanted to do something hard for our Lord's sake, he went to some holy place much as people do in these times. But there was a big difference: when we go to Lourdes, Croagh Patrick, or Lough Derg we go in a comfortable train or car; in the fifteenth century the pilgrim walked every step of the way. And there was another difference: we wear our ordinary clothes; the pilgrim of long ago dressed in a special way so that everyone would know at once what he was and what he was doing.

The pilgrim was known to be a quiet person doing something to please our Lord and not in the least likely to cause trouble or bother anyone.

Soldiers would let the pilgrim pass even if wars were being fought; no one questioned him or even spoke to him except to wish him the time of day and Godspeed.

The pilgrim always wore a habit, rather like the kind monks wear today; over the habit was a great cloak to keep out the wind and the rain; over all an enormous wide-brimmed hat tied with strings under the chin.

I greatly fear that if you were to see a pilgrim going along your road you would burst out laughing (he might laugh back at you, however, because you would look so funny to him in your modern clothes).

Pilgrims usually wore sandals (which are the best footwear for rough roads and smooth) and always had a leather bag tied to their belts. In the bag was a bottle of water, hunks of bread, holy medals, and perhaps a little money. Then there was the staff — a much stronger thing than the present-day walking stick — and, very important, the shell.

Now, a seashell (the kind used is called a scallop) might not seem very important to you but for the pilgrim it was very important: it was his badge. It told people what he was. So the scallop was sewn on to the pilgrim's shoulder and never left that place until the man came back home from the holy place where he was praying.

Now you know what the man hastening along the Italian road on the October evening looked like. He was dead tired and he walked as if every step hurt.

If you had seen this man you would have said that he was very old, but you would have been wrong. He wasn't old, he hadn't even reached middle life, but he was sick. Indeed, he was very ill, and ever since he had left the city gates he had been feeling worse: walking slower and slower, stopping every now and again to lean on his staff, gasping as sick people do.

It was growing quite dark; it was difficult to see the road at all. The man began to be sorry that he had left the city. He could have rested there; on the road there was no place to rest and no shelter. The houses were getting scarce, soon there would be none — but wait! He saw a fine house not so very far away. When he reached it he knocked at the door, praying that he would be let in.

"You are welcome here, stranger," said the person who answered the knock. "Would you like to have something for supper?"

The weary pilgrim was soon placed at a table and given food. Then he found out where he was. He had had the great luck (or answer to prayer, really) of chancing on a pilgrims' hostel where he could get supper and a nice clean bed — all for nothing.

There was a priest in charge of the hostel, a man who had given up his whole life to helping poor pilgrims on their hard way tramping to and from the holy places. When the tired pilgrim had finished his supper, he spent a little time talking with this kind priest.

When he heard that the hostel was founded by an Irish saint named Ursus, he was delighted and kept smiling without saying why he was smiling.

Then he went to bed; the priest urged him to do so because he looked so worn out and sick. No one asked him any questions about who he was, where he was going, or what he was doing. The man had the shell sewn on his shoulder and that told them all they needed to know.

Next morning, when the servants began to bustle round, beginning the work of the day, they were astonished to see a bright light shining from one of the rooms. They thought that a fire had broken out and they got excited.

They broke into the room prepared to put out the fire; but there was none. It was the room of the poor pilgrim who had arrived the night before. The light shone all around his bed. So they tried to wake him up so that he could explain this astonishing thing. But he wasn't asleep; he was dead.

The dead man's face was calm and peaceful and it had a look of enormous happiness. The other pilgrims crowded in from their rooms to see; the servants hurried off to call the priest. All the time the strange light shone around the bed, the brightest part of it seemed to come from the calm face.

When the priest came he was upset. Here was a stranger who died in their hostel and who had not received the Last Sacraments. The priest blamed himself but really he need not have done so because he hadn't known the stranger was so ill.

The Bishop happened to be living in the town near the hostel and a servant was sent for him. The Bishop looked long at the light-surrounded man while all the others stood by in silence.

"This is no ordinary man," said the Bishop. "He is somebody great. Let us examine what is in his bag to see if it will tell us who he is."

The pilgrims and servants left the room; the Bishop and priest searched the leather bag. There were the usual bottle of water and pieces of bread, but there were other things much more interesting. There were letters written and signed by the Pope, a gold cross, and a ring — a bishop's cross and ring.

They read the letters and found that the poor pilgrim was a bishop from Ireland named Thaddeus MacCarthy.

I wonder if they knew that Thaddeus MacCarthy was not only the head of the diocese of Cork but also a prince? The MacCarthy clan of Munster were, at one time, very powerful and in ancient times their head was given the honor of being king or prince.

The letters in Thaddeus's leather bag showed that he was on his way home from Rome to Ireland.

Well, the Bishop of Ivrea knew what to do then. First he sent word to the Pope that the Irish bishop was dead, and then he gave instructions on how the dead man was to be buried. The people of Ivrea dressed him in bishop's vestments and gave him the wonderful solemn funeral that bishops always have. "But this was no ordinary bishop," they said, just as their bishop had said, "This is no ordinary man."

The strangest things began to happen around his coffin in the church before the burial. Blind people passing it found that they could see; and deaf people, who had not heard a single whisper for years and years, found to their joy that once again they could hear everything. You can well imagine what happiness and excitement there was in Ivrea.

Many hundreds of years have now passed since the weary pilgrim stumbled into the hostel but even to this day in that city of North Italy people talk about Thaddeus MacCarthy. The Irish bishop was both holy and humble. Bishops, even in those far-off times, did not go about in large hats tied under the chin; they did not walk the lonely roads all by themselves. Usually bishops had servants and a secretary going about with them; people bowed to them and said, "My Lord," and went down on one knee and kissed the bishop's ring. Thaddeus kept his ring in the bag at his belt where it jostled against the water bottle and the bread.

How very differently Thaddeus would have been received at the pilgrims' hostel if he had worn his cross and ring and held out the interesting letters from the Pope! Probably they would have made a big fuss and led the Irish bishop right off to their own bishop where he would have had the best of everything. Thaddeus hadn't wanted that. He was a true pilgrim; he wanted to do the humble and the hard thing; he thought a great deal about how he looked in God's eyes, but nothing at all about how he looked in the eyes of men.

It was a long time before the news came to Ireland that Thaddeus MacCarthy was dead. He had gone to Rome to see the Pope about something, he was making a pilgrimage, and he never came back. There were bad times in Ireland then and Catholics were everywhere suffering death and torture for the Faith; perhaps the unhappy Irish people could spare little time to think of their missing bishop because of the terrible troubles they had at home.

At any rate it was not until hundreds of years afterward, when the whole story of Thaddeus MacCarthy's holy death was known, that a bishop of Cork went over to Italy and brought back relics of Blessed Thaddeus for Cork Cathedral.

It must be nice to be a Tighe, Tadhg, or Thady, or to be a MacCarthy because your saint is honored in two great Catholic countries: Italy and Ireland.

know many children who are afraid of the dark and who have to have a little light left burning in their room all night. I know others who are afraid even to hear about witches, or giants, or ghosts — especially ghosts. I know others who are afraid of beardy old men of the roads. I know a small boy who is so afraid of tinkers that when he is coming home from school by himself, he peeps round every corner first in case he sees one. Well, if you're like that, St. Gall is the man for you. He wasn't afraid of anything under the sun.

St. Gall was one of the twelve monks who left Ireland with St. Columbanus to work as missionaries in France and Italy. While they were on that long journey, Gall became ill in Switzerland, so ill that it was impossible for him to travel any farther. Columbanus had to leave him behind in the care of a priest whom they met on their way.

Very slowly Gall got better from his illness. As he lay in bed he kept thinking of his companions, who were, by this time, preaching the good news of God to pagan people.

"But," said he to himself, "the people here in Switzerland are pagan, too. Instead of following Columbanus into Italy, I will stay here and preach to the Swiss." And so he did. It was thus by an accident that Gall became the Apostle of Switzerland.

He told his plan to the priest. "I want," he said, "to remain here and teach the Swiss people about God, just as Patrick taught the Irish." The priest thought this was a great idea. Gall then said that he would like to move into the middle of the country, build a monastery there, and start teaching.

The trouble was that he didn't know the country because he had been ill ever since he came. The priest promised to send a man with him who knew every inch of the country and so could help Gall to find a nice place in which to build a church and house.

As soon as Gall was well enough to travel, he set off with this young man for a guide. He was a pleasant young fellow, but not very brave — certainly not as brave as Gall. They traveled on foot for a whole day, and as they walked, they passed the time talking of the best kind of a place for a monastery.

"It should have good soil," said Gall, "so that I can till and sow it. I must have corn and vegetables to feed the monks and the people who will come to learn from me."

"What else?" asked the guide.

"Water, too, of course," said Gall. "It should have a spring of good water because we could not live without pure water to drink."

"And what else?" asked the guide again.

"It would have to be level ground," said Gall, "because it is too hard to dig the land on hilly places and a slope would make building harder too."

"Is that all?" asked the guide.

"Well, I'd like beautiful scenery too," said Gall, "because that helps to lift the mind to God."

Just as he was saying this, Gall's foot caught in a bramble which tripped him so that he fell flat on the ground.

The guide ran to help him, but Gall, instead of jumping up and rubbing the dirt from himself, just knelt upright and began a long prayer of thanksgiving. When at last he stood up, he said to the guide, "This is the very place I want."

"Oh, no!" said the guide, "this won't do at all."

"Why not?" asked Gall.

"Well, do you see those forests and rocks all around us?" said the guide, looking frightened. "They're full of wild animals of the worst kind: bears, fierce wolves, wild boars, and poisonous snakes. You couldn't possibly live in a place like this."

"Oh, I don't mind wild animals at all," Gall said, smiling. "They'll do me no harm."

He stood up and walked to the nearest tree from which he cut two branches and tied them together in the form of a cross. He stuck this upright on the ground to mark the place where he had tripped.

"Here I remain," he said. "With God's help, my church and my house will be here."

They then prepared to camp for the night. They lit a big fire, near which they meant to sleep. Beside them ran a clear stream, forming a deep pool some distance away. Gall had brought a small net with him, folded into his wallet. He shook this out now and began to fish in the pool. Soon he had a few lovely fish which they cooked for their supper and ate with the bread they had brought with them.

They were quite happy until darkness began to fall. Then the guide got awfully nervous, thinking of all the wild animals in the surrounding forest. He thought to himself, "They'll come out and devour us." But he said nothing more about it to Gall, because he knew well the saint would only say, "God will take care of us."

The two men said their prayers and lay down to sleep. The fire they had built made a little circle of light in the darkness.

When Gall thought his companion was fast asleep, he got up again very carefully, trying not to make any sound that would wake the other. He walked over to the cross he had planted in the ground and he knelt down there and began to pray again for the success of his great plan. The guide pretended he was asleep, but he was watching all the time. He was too frightened to sleep because he could hear the wolves howling in the forest and the sound made him shake with fear.

Presently there was a shuffling noise and into the circle of firelight walked a huge bear. The guide's heart seemed to jump into his throat and he was so terrified that he could not speak even to warn Gall, who had his back turned to the animal. "We're lost," thought the guide. "It's all up with us now."

The bear began to nose around on the spot where the two men had had their supper. He was interested in the remains of fish and bread on the ground and began to lick them up. Gall now heard it, and turned to look.

The guide expected him to give a scream of fright, but instead he said in the most gentle and friendly way, "Hello, bear, please put a piece of wood on that fire for me."

The bear obeyed. Shuffling in his awkward way, he got hold of a log in his forepaws, and settled it neatly on the dying fire. Then Gall took half a loaf of bread out of his wallet and gave it to the bear, who sat back contentedly on his haunches while he ate it. As he was eating, Gall talked to him.

"I'll share this wild, desert place with you on condition that you do no harm to my men or my cattle, when I have them."

The bear grunted and went on eating the bread. He liked the bread and he liked Gall but all the same he walked off again into the forest as soon as he had finished. No sooner was he gone than the guide jumped up and ran to Gall, threw himself at his feet and said, "Now I know that you are indeed a man of God, when even the wild animals obey you."

Gall carried out his plan. He built his church and house in that spot where they had camped and no wild animals ever harmed him or his followers.

To this day St. Gall is greatly honored by the Swiss; everywhere in that country of Alps and snow are pictures of St. Gall and the bear. Sometimes the bear is shown lying at the saint's feet, or else the bear may be shown standing on its hind legs with a piece of wood in its forepaws. You can buy little bears holding logs as a souvenir of your holiday in Switzerland.

There is a great Swiss town called St. Gallen after our Irish St. Gall. It is a nice thought that it was an Irishman who first brought Christianity to faraway Switzerland.

his is the last and shortest story in the book. It should take you only a minute to read it, but I am not so sure; minutes have a funny way of flying. Sad minutes and pain minutes crawl like snails; happy minutes go like the wind. My story is about minutes that go like the wind.

Listen: one April day long, long ago the Abbot of a monastery sent all the monks to work in a nearby wood. A new church was being built and there was urgent need of timber and wattles.

One young monk, the man of this story, was told to bring back a load of wattles. It was hard work cutting the wattles — thin branches that can be woven together for walls or fences — and loading them on the cart, but by evening the job was finished.

The young monk sat down for a short rest. The sun was setting and the sky was filled with brilliant colors; the starry blossoms of the blackthorns were made rosy by the sunlight; the grassy bank where he sat was dotted with primroses.

How sweetly the birds sang, how fresh and scented the evening air! He was very content. Then a special bird began to sing in an especially lovely way: clear, flutelike notes rising and falling, rilling and trilling — so lovely as almost to hurt the heart. The young monk was very happy; he felt that he would never weary of the bird's song.

"You had a hard day's work, Young Monk."

"I had to work hard," replied the monk very seriously, "because we are building a church here in honor of the good God."

Then, suddenly, he thought it strange that he was talking to a bird and, far stranger, that a bird had talked to him! "Who, may I ask, are you?" he politely asked the bird.

"I am an angel sent from God," replied the bird.

"Indeed, I salute you, Angel," said the monk. "But why did you come here to talk to me?"

"God sent me," replied the angel bird, "because you did a hard day's work for Him. I am to amuse you for a little while, God said."

And so they talked of Heaven, the beauty and goodness of God, His Holy Mother, the angels, and saints. It was a happy talk and when the angel bird said good-bye the Young Monk was sad. But he returned to the load of wattles and started to go home.

When he reached the monastery, the church was built. He looked around at the monks. They were all strangers. He stopped one of them and asked where his own friends were. The man looked surprised and then said that all those men the Young Monk spoke of were long since dead: he had spent one hundred and fifty years listening to the singing of a bird.

ABOUT THE SAINTS

Adamnan (c. 624–704) also called Eunan. He wrote an important biography of Columcille and preserved the stories of others of his time. His feast is September 23rd.

Benignus (died 467) also called Benen. His father was the Irish chieftain Sesenen. Benignus's feast is November 9th.

Brendan (488–c. 577) called Brendan the Navigator or the Voyager. He helped establish numerous monastic communities throughout Ireland and founded the diocese of Clonfert in County Galway. His feast is November 29th.

Brigid (c. 451–525) also called Bridget. She founded a convent and a monastery in Kildare which became a center of religion and learning. Her feast is January 21st.

Canice (c. 515–599) also called Kenny, Kenneth, and Cainnech. He studied under Finnian at Clonard and was a close friend of Columcille. Canice's feast is October 11th.

Ciaran (died c. 530) also called Kieran of Saighir and Kieran the Elder. He was a hermit before becoming the first bishop of Ossory. His feast is March 5th.

Colman of Kilmacduagh (died c. 632) founded the monastery of Kilmacduagh. His feast is October 29th.

Colman-Elo (c. 555–611) also called Colman of Lann Elo and Colman Mascusailni. He was the author of *The Alphabet of Devotion*. Columcille was his uncle. Colman-Elo's feast is September 26th.

Columbanus (c. 540–615) also called Columban. With Gall and several other companions, he traveled extensively, preaching and founding monasteries. His feast is November 23rd.

Columcille (521–597) also called Columba of Iona, Colm, and Colum. He helped set up communities in Derry, Durrow, and Kells before founding his monastery on the island of Iona off the coast of Scotland. His feast is June 9th.

Cormac (6th century) was a sailor and a contemporary of Columcille and Adamnan. We have his story through some of Adamnan's writings. Cormac's feast is September 14th.

Finbarr (died c. 633) also called Lochan, Fionbarr, Barr, and Bairre. He was the first bishop of Cork. His feast is September 25th.

Finnian (c. 470–c. 549) "the teacher of the Irish saints," also called Finnian of Clonard. He founded many schools, churches, and monasteries. His feast is December 12th.

Flannan (7th century) is the patron saint and first bishop of Killaloe. His feast is December 18th.

Gall (died c. 635) traveled through Europe as a missionary with Columbanus and his companions, and is famous as the "apostle of Switzerland." He was also a scholar and helped to found Luxeuil Monastery. His feast is October 16th.

MacCarthy, Thaddeus (died 1492), also called Tadhg, was beatified in 1895. His feast is kept on October 25th in the dioceses of Ross, Cork, and Cloyne, in Ireland, and in Ivrea, Italy, where he died and was buried.

Modomnoc (6th century) is sometimes called Domnoc or Dominic, and is said to have introduced bees to Ireland. His feast is February 13th.

O'Toole, Laurence (1128–1180), also called Lawrence and Lorcan Ó Tuathail, became Archbishop of Dublin and later died in Eu, France, trying to make peace between England and Ireland. He was canonized in 1227.

Patrick (c. 389–c. 461) is the most famous of all the Irish saints. His feast is March 17th.

About the Author

Alice Curtayne (1901–1981) was born in Country Kerry, Ireland, married fellow author Stephen Rynne in 1935, and with him raised a family on their farm in County Kildare, Ireland.

She frequently visited the United States on lecture tours and wrote a novel, historical surveys of Ireland, numerous biographies, and two collections of Irish saints' stories for children.

An Invitation

Reader, the book that you hold in your hands was published by Sophia Institute Press. Sophia Institute seeks to nurture the spiritual, moral, and cultural life of souls and to spread the Gospel of Christ in conformity with the authentic teachings of the Roman Catholic Church.

Our press fulfills this mission by offering translations, reprints, and new publications that afford readers a rich source of the enduring wisdom of mankind.

We also operate two popular online Catholic resources: CrisisMagazine.com and CatholicExchange.com.

Crisis Magazine provides insightful cultural analysis that arms readers with the arguments necessary for navigating the ideological and theological minefields of the day. *Catholic Exchange* provides world news from a Catholic perspective as well as daily devotionals and articles that will help you to grow in holiness and live a life consistent with the teachings of the Church.

Sophia Institute Press also serves as the publisher for the Thomas More College of Liberal Arts and Holy Spirit College. Both colleges provide university-level education under the guiding light of Catholic teaching. If you know a young person seeking a college that takes seriously the adventure of learning and the quest for truth, please bring these institutions to his attention.

www.SophiaInstitute.com
www.CatholicExchange.com
www.CrisisMagazine.com

Sophia Institute Press® is a registered trademark of Sophia Institute.
Sophia Institute is a tax-exempt institution as defined by the Internal Revenue Code, Section 501(c)(3). Tax I.D. 22-2548708.